HD62.15 .C487 2012
The power of LEO :
33663005344771
HLC

DATE DUE

Praise for *The Power of LEO*

Nobody knows quality like Subir Chowdhury, and The Power of LEO *reveals the elegant new approach he has pioneered with the world's top companies. I couldn't recommend this book more.*

—Marshall Goldsmith
Author of the *New York Times* bestsellers *MOJO* and
What Got You Here Won't Get You There

The Power of LEO *will be beneficial to any organization that utilizes the principles and incorporates it into their culture. Subir Chowdhury's LEO is guaranteed to produce results.*

—Michael King
CEO and National President, Volunteers of America

Subir Chowdhury is one of the world's leading experts on quality improvement, and he's on a mission to instill that same passionate dedication in every person at every level. In The Power of LEO *he goes a long way to doing just that. It's a no-nonsense book full of real-life case examples, practical tips, and proven strategies. If you're looking to make quality a way of life, this is definitely the book for you.*

—Jim Kouzes
Coauthor of the bestselling *The Leadership Challenge*
The Dean's Executive Fellow of Leadership
Leavey School of Business, Santa Clara University

Subir brings forward a fresh perspective on managing global corpora-
tions by listening carefully to key stakeholders, enriching critical business
processes, and optimizing the strategic change initiatives for deriving
maximum business value. In an uncomplicated style, he uses multiple
case studies to explain how the LEO management approach can solve
significant business challenges. Avid readers of new ideas in manage-
ment techniques would certainly find this work of interest.

—Narayana N. R. Murthy
Chairman and Chief Mentor, Infosys Limited

The Power of LEO *highlights the importance of improving process de-*
sign in any industry, including health care. We have applied LEO in my
hospital and it works. Subir Chowdhury's book will serve as a powerful
reminder to the health care industry that its primary goal is to develop,
enhance, and delight its most important customer: the patient.

—Mark L. Rosenblum, M.D.
Chair, Department of Neurosurgery, Henry Ford Health System
Vice President of Clinical Programs, Henry Ford West
Bloomfield Hospital

The Power of LEO *has rekindled my belief in the value of listening to*
and collaborating with all of our stakeholders.

—James E. Rogers
Chairman, President, and CEO, Duke Energy

Most management strategies are great in theory. But how does a line
executive put it to use? The Power of LEO *shows us how in practical,*
down-to-earth terms and anecdotes. A most useful read!

—Jim Lawrence
CEO, Rothschild North America and Former Vice Chairman
and CFO, General Mills

THE
POWER
OF
LEO

THE
POWER
OF
LEO

**THE REVOLUTIONARY PROCESS
FOR ACHIEVING
EXTRAORDINARY RESULTS**

SUBIR CHOWDHURY

NEW YORK   CHICAGO   SAN FRANCISCO
LISBON   LONDON   MADRID   MEXICO CITY   MILAN
NEW DELHI   SAN JUAN   SEOUL   SINGAPORE
SYDNEY   TORONTO

The **McGraw·Hill** Companies

1 2 3 4 5 6 7 8 9 0   DOC/DOC   1 6 5 4 3 2 1

ISBN: 978-0-07-176799-6
MHID: 0-07-176799-1

e-ISBN 978-0-07-176995-2
e-MHID   0-07-176995-1

Design by Mauna Eichner and Lee Fukui

This publication is designed to provide accurate and authoritative information in regard to the subject matter covered. It is sold with the understanding that neither the author nor the publisher is engaged in rendering legal, accounting, securities trading, or other professional service. If legal advice or other expert assistance is required, the services of a competent professional person should be sought.

>—*From a Declaration of Principles Jointly Adopted by a Committee of the American Bar Association and a Committee of Publishers and Associations*

Library of Congress Cataloging-in-Publication Data

Chowdhury, Subir.
  The power of LEO : the revolutionary process for achieving extraordinary results / by Subir Chowdhury.
      p. cm.
  Includes bibliographical references.
  ISBN-13: 978-0-07-176799-6 (alk. paper)
  ISBN-10: 0-07-176799-1 (alk. paper)
  1. Total quality management. 2. Quality control. 3. Management. 4. Organizational effectiveness. I. Title.
  HD62.15.C487 2012
  658.4'013--dc23

                                                                    2011033641

LEO® is a registered Trademark of Subir Chowdhury

In memory of my father,
Sushil Kumar Chowdhury

CONTENTS

CONTENTS

PREFACE

On April 3, 1973, Marty Cooper almost became the first person with a mobile phone plastered to his ear to be hit by a car. He was so busy talking, so excited about what he was doing, that he stepped out into a New York City street without looking.

His excitement was understandable. He was making the first-ever public call on a handheld mobile phone, the device he had been shepherding through the systems division at Motorola. It weighed in at 2.2 pounds. The battery lasted only 20 minutes, but that wasn't a major problem, he said, "because you couldn't hold that phone up for that long."

Until then, mobile phones had been bulky objects on the dashboards of cars, requiring all sorts of equipment elsewhere in the vehicles. But when Cooper took over the division that produced the car phones, he became, as he put it, "a zealot" for portability. He announced a contest within Motorola for a design for a mobile phone. He chose the simplest design, had it built and tested within a few months, and went public with it on that April day outside the Hilton Hotel.

Marty Cooper's historic coup enabled Motorola to dominate the early cell phone market for years, but the company was slow to switch from analog to digital devices and to provide user-friendly models. Market leadership passed from Motorola and other U.S. manufacturers to foreign competitors. Today, the top three cell phone makers are Nokia, Samsung, and LG Electronics.

And that was how yet another American invention has ended up filling the coffers of our overseas rivals. Everything from the television set to the windshield wiper, from the microwave oven to the handheld calculator to solar panel technology, has followed that same path.

I was not born in the United States. I chose to make my home and my life here. I love this country. And I have watched with sadness and anger as we have yielded competitive advantage to China and other developing countries. True, we still lead in innovation, and we still get to market first, but within a matter of months after our products hit the shelves, our overseas rivals are eating our lunch.

When I ask myself why that is so, the answer seems clear: these competitors have been able to build quality into *our* inventions. They seize upon our new products and make them better in every way—simpler, easier to use, and less expensive. We no longer know how to get it right the first time. The hard truth is that America is engaged in a global quality war—and we're losing.

When I meet with CEOs and senior leaders across the globe, I find that very few of them practice *quality* as a strategy. Yes, they give it lip service. Ask any manager on any level in any company, large or small, and you will get the same response: "Quality is our core strategy." In many organizations, they will offer more evidence of their commitment: "After all, don't we have a vice president of quality? Don't we have a quality department?"

But right there, in a few words, is the answer to what's wrong. Quality should be—and must be—everyone's business if we are to realize our potential and gain back the ground that we've lost in the quality war. We as managers must, individually, take responsibility for the quality mission and stop delegating it to some other person or department. It must rule every aspect of our operations, permanently lodged within the core of our corporate culture.

Gary Hirshberg, CEO of Stonyfield Farm, a pioneer in organic foods, said it well: "Quality, quality, quality: never waver from it, even when you don't see how you can afford to keep it up. When you compromise, you become a commodity, and then you die."

This book offers a powerful new management approach that can help us achieve quality at all levels of the organization. It represents a significant departure from past practice, gradually evolving as my colleagues and I have taken part in management improvement projects over the years. We call it LEO, which stands for Listen, Enrich, and Optimize, and it has been applied, in whole or in part, at dozens of organizations ranging from small nonprofits to Fortune 500 behemoths.

As you will see in the pages ahead, it works.

LEO made its first appearance in print in 2005, when I published *The Ice Cream Maker*, a small story about Pete, the plant manager of a struggling dairy company, who was trying to sell his ice cream line to Mike, the manager of the local branch of a national chain of grocery stores. In the course of 115 pages, Mike helps Pete put the principles of LEO to work at his dairy: Listen to your customers, Enrich the products or services that you offer, and Optimize the customer experience. Pete goes on to transform his dairy's operations and products—and win Mike as a customer.

In some ways, the book was a far cry from any of my previous works, all of them serious discussions of complex management systems such as Six Sigma and Design for Six Sigma. What they all had in common, though, was a deep and abiding concern for quality. Once we had developed the LEO approach, I wrote *The Ice Cream Maker* as a way to carry its quality message to people of every kind in every type of work, from the boardroom to the assembly line.

That little book came to be embraced by people in all walks of life around the world, and I began to receive calls and e-mails from businesspeople and nonprofit organizations saying how intrigued they were by the LEO methodology. But many of them also had a request. "In *The Ice Cream Maker*, you've given us a 30,000-foot look at LEO," they'd say. "How about bringing it down to 5,000 feet?" I had the same answer for all of them: "Before I write any serious business book about LEO, I want to see how it actually works when it is implemented. Is it delivering a quality culture change? Is it really better at solving problems and enriching products?"

Once LEO had proved itself over and over again with companies of every size and every variety, I felt it was time to respond to that request. This book is the result. In easy-to-understand, nontechnical language, it clearly explains LEO for a business audience and shows how LEO can be and has been used to great advantage in real, down-to-earth business situations. I sincerely hope that you will find the book of value, both as a window into the operations of other businesses and as a collection of ideas that you will want to take back to your own organization to share with your colleagues and friends.

Subir Chowdhury
subir.chowdhury@asiusa.com
www.subirchowdhury.com
Bloomfield Hills, Michigan

Chapter One

INTRODUCING LEO

Back in 2003, the chief executive of a large East Coast hospital invited me to an 11 a.m. meeting with him and his leadership team. "We have a problem," he began. The organization had gone through weeks of training in Six Sigma with the goal of trimming waste and boosting efficiency. But six months later, the results were meager. He wanted to know if I could help.

In the course of our talk, I asked each of the six executives what I thought was a simple question: "You learned a lot of tool sets during your training, so tell me what percentage of them you've been able to apply in your work." The answers shook me. "Fifty percent," said the chief medical officer. "Thirty percent," said the CFO. All six of them had the same basic response: a huge chunk of the Six Sigma tools they had spent so much time learning was simply inappropriate to their needs.

It's ironic in a way. At a time in history when we have, more than ever, an abundance of impressive management tools to help us seriously ratchet up performance, most of us have made only marginal gains. Lean manufacturing, reengineering, Total Quality Management, Six Sigma: on and on the list goes. A handful of inspired leaders—Jack Welch of General Electric comes to mind—have made the most of these tools. But many companies have invested huge amounts of time, energy, and cash in them without significantly improving the quality of their operations.

After the meeting with the hospital leaders, I called my own team together. Now I was the one saying, "We have a problem." Like the rest of the management community, we had been automatically introducing the whole gamut of Six Sigma and the other management tools into companies without having an in-depth understanding of the companies' goals, their cultures, or their core strengths and weaknesses. "We have to change," I said. "We have to start tailoring the tools to fit each company's circumstances." No more cookie-cutter presentations for us.

That was when we began to develop the management approach that we now call LEO, for Listen, Enrich, and Optimize, and we have spent all the years since then putting it to the test in one organization after another. It has passed with flying colors, because LEO is not simply another management tool; rather, it is an overall methodology that makes it possible to apply management tools to maximum advantage. In other words, LEO represents a new mindset, a transformational way to think about the decisions that managers on every level make and the actions that they take. It is a system devised to help companies dramatically improve their performance, to make quality part of their corporate DNA.

LEO represents a new mindset, a transformational way to think about the decisions that managers on every level make and the actions that they take.

When I go to visit a company today, I explain the LEO strategy. I assure the leaders that whatever suggestions we make, and whatever management tools we employ, will be geared precisely to their company's special needs and particular makeup. If they follow the LEO methodology, they will achieve a major, measurable increase in the quality of their operations, their products, and their bottom line.

In the chapters ahead, I explain the various aspects of LEO in detail. I also show through case histories how it has actually been implemented, although the names of the companies described and sometimes the products or services that they provide have been altered to protect their confidentiality. Right now, though, I would like to introduce you to the basic elements of the LEO strategy:

- **LISTEN: Observe and Understand.** To obtain a deep comprehension of the issue at hand, put aside past assumptions and interact directly with all relevant parties—specifically including customers, suppliers, and employees. Add to your findings whatever relevant data can be uncovered.

  One of a company's two call centers was experiencing many more database-entry errors than the other. Company managers suspected that it was a training problem, assuming that the errors were concentrated in the third shift, where most new hires were assigned. We began the Listen process with intense data mining of the center's records. When we analyzed the figures, we discovered that most of the errors were in fact committed during the first shift and were clustered in a single row of 20 workstations—a row that was next to the windows. The glare from the windows was making it difficult for workers to see their screens clearly. Our suggestion that the company cover the windows was vetoed by the public relations department, which led frequent tours through the center. Instead, tinted window glass was installed and glare filters were added to each workstation. Entry errors were reduced by 95 percent.

- **ENRICH: Explore and Discover.** Based upon the information you have gathered, reach out to all relevant parties for ideas and possible solutions. The wider you cast your net, the more likely it is that you will move beyond the usual suspects to discover new and better answers.

At a hospital division serving the elderly with neurological problems such as Parkinson's or dementia, we discovered in the Listen process that many patients had to go through three to six weeks of tests and waiting for results before a diagnosis could be delivered. If a patient arrived complaining of dizziness, say, she might be tested for an inner ear infection; if the results were negative, she would be tested in the next day or two for another possible cause; and so it went as the weeks passed. Based on our observations and numerous interviews with patients and staff members, we created a detailed map of the existing process, identifying areas of waste and inefficiency. With that laid out in front of us, we entered the Enrich phase of LEO, using analytical tools to develop new and improved patient flow.

Today, after an in-depth interview with a geriatrician, patients are given a series of basic tests on the first day that cover most conditions. Then all of their doctors get together to consider the results and jointly arrive at a diagnosis and treatment plan. Their conclusions are passed on to the patients by a neurologist or geriatrician. The whole process can take as little as two days.

- **OPTIMIZE: Improve and Perfect.** Examine the solutions you have found and select the best. Subject it to every kind of challenge it might conceivably encounter, and correct any and all possible shortcomings.

When a new application was found for its electric motor, a company's engineers would come up with a design and put the result through a 12-week process to make sure it worked properly. If it failed the evaluation, they would come up with another design and go through the whole process again. We suggested another approach that is part of LEO's Optimize phase. Instead of focusing on the nuts and bolts of a particular design, we turned our attention to the essential purpose of the motor—to transform electricity into torque, causing a shaft to turn. We eventually found that by closely measuring the efficiency of that transformation under various

> *conditions, we could accurately predict whether a new design would pass the evaluation process. Now, rather than putting a new design through a dozen weeks of testing, the engineers can determine its quality in all of 10 minutes.*

By rigorously and consistently using one or all of the LEO guidelines, these three companies achieved far higher levels of performance, thereby measurably enhancing their products, services, and finances. That's because LEO can find answers to the questions that plague managers everywhere: Why are my sales dropping off? What can I do about my excessive scrap? How do I reduce high turnover? How can I match my competitor's price? Why is my new product pipeline empty? How can I get to best in class in my industry?

In the final analysis, though, the answers to all these questions boil down to one word: *quality*. The unending pursuit of quality, of perfection, is the single most important action any individual or organization can take to resolve problems and achieve goals.

We all know quality when we see it. I think of the performance I attended by Ravi Shankar, the great Indian composer and sitar virtuoso. He was 88 years old at that time, but the standard he set for himself and the musicians who accompanied him never flagged. Show or no show, if their playing was anything less than perfect, Shankar's eyes would blaze at them. Quality above all.

The unending pursuit of quality, of perfection, is the single most important action any individual or organization can take to resolve problems and achieve goals.

Sadly, the striving for perfection that used to be the hallmark of American business has fallen away in recent years, and our economy has paid the price. The loss of quality is manifest in every aspect of our personal and business lives.

Not long ago, I purchased two books and an audio CD on Amazon.com. When my order arrived, the CD was missing, even though the shipping slip listed all three items. After spending 15 minutes searching the site for a telephone number to call, I reached a customer service representative. He listened to my tale and immediately promised to have the missing CD mailed to me, no questions asked. That led me to inquire whether this sort of mistake happens frequently. "From time to time," he replied. "It's human error."

I don't doubt that Amazon, like most consumer outfits, tries to avoid such errors. Yet all of us are constantly encountering something similar in our dealings with merchants of every kind. It's annoying, and it's a symptom of the quality failures that are plaguing our country. And when those failures occur on a larger scale, it can be frightening.

Ever since a 1999 report by the Institute of Medicine found that medical mistakes in hospitals caused up to 98,000 deaths a year, leaders of the medical profession have initiated dozens of projects to improve patient safety.

Some hospitals set up computerized drug-ordering systems to reduce medication errors. Others instituted programs to cut back on infections, including the installation of waterless antiseptic hand washes. The schedules of interns were rearranged to avoid the sleep deprivation that can lead to medical error.

But the results have been minimal. One investigation, released in 2010, of 10 hospitals in North Carolina found that there had been no appreciable lowering of patient injuries between 2002 and

2007—even though North Carolina had been selected for the study because its hospitals were in the forefront of the patient safety movement. According to a federal report dealing with Medicare hospital patients for the month of October 2008, 13.5 percent of them experienced "adverse events," meaning medical errors. In the case of 1.5 percent of the patients, some 15,000 people, those errors contributed to their deaths.

In a 2010 interview with the *New York Times*, Dr. Robert M. Wachter, chief of hospital medicine at the University of California, San Francisco, summed up the prospects for greater patient safety:

> Process changes, like a new computer system or the use of a checklist, may help a bit, but if they are not embedded in a system in which the providers are engaged in safety efforts, educated about how to identify safety hazards and fix them, and have a culture of strong communication and teamwork, progress may be painfully slow.[*]

In other words, you're not going to achieve real quality piecemeal. It requires an organization's total and continuing commitment to the cause. The ancient Greek philosopher Aristotle said it best: "Quality is not an act, it is a habit."

THE FOUR CORNERSTONES

There are many paths to quality. LEO projects, for example, may take a month, a few years—or anywhere in between. They may be

---

[*] Denise Gray, "Study Finds No Progress in Safety at Hospitals," *New York Times*, November 2, 2010, p. A1.

limited to a single area of an organization or include the organization as a whole—or anywhere in between. It all depends upon the degree to which the management wants to commit to the Listen, Enrich, and Optimize approach. Sometimes companies start small, are impressed by the results, and then decide to go for a wholesale deployment.

For organizations that make a major commitment to LEO, their success will be determined in large measure by the level of their commitment to four basic principles. We call them *cornerstones* because the more closely you abide by them, the more your total LEO experience will align with your expectations.

The attitudes expressed in the four cornerstones are not arbitrary; they are carefully considered and essential elements of the LEO approach. Once they are embedded in any organization's culture, its quality will soar.

1. Quality Is My Responsibility

The next time someone stands up at a meeting and talks about quality, listen carefully to the attendees' reactions. Chances are they will be all about what other people can do to improve things. One person will want to refer the matter to the Quality department. Another person will shrug, saying that it's an operational issue that's best left to Engineering. That attitude defeats any possibility of achieving a quality transformation.

The pursuit of quality must be a personal responsibility, reflected in every aspect of your work. When you make a decision, do you ask yourself whether it will improve your customers' experience with the company? Do you consider whether it will improve your employees' motivation? Do you ponder whether it will advance the quality initiative?

9

The pursuit of quality must be a personal responsibility, reflected in every aspect of your work.

Those are the same kind of searching questions we are all learning to ask ourselves about the environment: Are we recycling our glass and paper? Are we picking up after our dogs or turning off the sprinkler overnight? We recognize the need to be personally responsible for the environment. LEO calls upon us to do the same for our organizations. I say, let everyone become her own quality department. I say, quality is *my* responsibility.

Responsibility carries with it accountability, and a LEO organization has no room for the blame game, the shunting of your responsibility for error onto others. Accountability without responsibility is morally repugnant and counterproductive, poisoning an organization's relationships and culture. Doing your job to the best of your ability is the starting point. Learning from your mistakes, doing your job right, and then finding new ways to do it better— that's the LEO way.

2. All the People, All the Time

How often have you been in a public space that sports an overflowing trash can? At the end of the day, the janitor walks in and picks up the overflow, and he is likely to do that very same thing every day until he retires. A bigger trash can would make his job easier

10

and greatly improve the looks of the place, but it never happens. The janitor never even considers the idea, and even if he did, he most likely would never bother to suggest it to his boss. Why? "It's not my job," he'd say.

In a LEO deployment, it becomes his job. There is no way a company can attain quality without the dedication of the whole universe of its stakeholders—every supplier and distributor as well as every manager and frontline worker. The quality mission belongs to all the people, all the time.

Leaders have a special duty to constantly reinforce that message by delivering it in every meeting and every encounter with their reports and by walking the talk, demonstrating their personal commitment to quality in their own work lives. For example, at your meetings, do you make sure that everyone has a chance to speak her mind? It's a hallmark of the LEO approach. And if you make it clear that you consider it to be important, your aides will pass that behavior down through the ranks.

The quality mission belongs to all the people, all the time.

Employees on every level are to be treated as full partners in the quality campaign, regularly encouraged to continuously improve their own performance and share their ideas for improving other operations. Their contributions toward greater quality need to be acknowledged and, where appropriate, amply rewarded.

3. An I-Can-Do-It Mindset

A salesperson had to meet with a customer in another state. But before she could buy the airline ticket, she told me, she had to get four levels of managers to sign off on the trip. I know of one company that actually requires a vice president's signature.

Any management that is so insecure about and untrusting of its employees is not going to receive the benefit of its workers' best performance or fresh insights. If you treat an associate like a child, don't expect him to behave like an independent-minded, responsibility-seeking adult.

There's a straight line between leaders' policies and the behavior and attitudes of their workers—and between those attitudes and the company's quality quotient. In a LEO deployment, management needs to build up employees' confidence in themselves and their readiness to take part in the quality transformation.

That means talking to your boss about *your role* in LEO and the aspects you feel secure about, and also those that you're unsure of. It means conducting similar discussions with your reports, helping them with aspects they don't understand and inspiring them to have a can-do attitude toward LEO. Managers and line people alike need to be encouraged to think and act outside the box.

In all your efforts to boost the confidence of those around you, the single most important way to inspire them is to demonstrate your own confidence and can-do attitude in your daily behavior.

Of course, in all your efforts to boost the confidence of those around you, the single most important way to inspire them is to demonstrate your own confidence and can-do attitude in your daily behavior.

4. No One Size Fits All

It's always tempting to look for a policy or a procedure that can be applied across the board to any and all situations. It would make life so much simpler. But too often, such solutions prove counterproductive. There are so many special cases and exceptions that, in fact, one size never comes very close to fitting all. The result: lots of confusion and waste.

That unhappy scenario often plays out when a company takes on a quality program like Six Sigma, which is typically applied in a strict, no-exceptions manner. By the same token, copying a quality program that was a smash hit at another company rarely succeeds, and can actually lower your quality level.

Every organization is unique. Even within the same industry, even within the same locale, no two companies will have matching management skills, corporate cultures, or talent bases. Just as the transfusion of the wrong blood type can devastate a person, the infusion of the wrong management program can cripple an organization. A LEO deployment recognizes the absolute necessity of tailoring solutions to the specific needs of the particular company. If an organization has already been trained in Six Sigma tools, for example, the deployment would blend the appropriate Six Sigma tools into the LEO program.

A LEO deployment recognizes the absolute necessity of tailoring solutions to the specific needs of the particular company.

The no-one-size-fits-all principle is also a guide to relationships during a LEO project. Leaders on all levels need to avoid automatic, knee-jerk responses to issues arising from the quality campaign. The way you've always handled a situation in the past may not be appropriate in a LEO environment. Initiatives and reactions need to be considered solely in terms of whether they advance or hold back the thrust toward greater quality—that is the new metric.

MOVING FORWARD WITH LEO

In the chapter just ahead, you will learn how LEO is used to deal with the various kinds of challenges that managers confront in their everyday business lives. I will describe and display the basics of LEO, providing insight into this effective method. You will also see LEO coping with a nuts-and-bolts problem that was slowing the pace of recovery from a natural disaster.

Throughout the rest of the chapters, case studies will provide not only anecdotal stories but also hard facts on how LEO deployments work, what kinds of problems they have been used to solve, and what types of outcomes can be expected.

Remember: Listen, Enrich, and Optimize.

Chapter Two

LEO AT WORK

It's a simple question. Which makes better sense—to invest time and energy in avoiding problems or in solving them? Too many companies get the answer wrong.

Managers complain that they're so busy jumping from one crisis to another that they're lucky if they can get their regular jobs done. They say they can't even consider taking the time to rethink the way they work in order to cut back on those crises. That whole frame of mind is aided and abetted by top management, which makes a fuss over the firefighters and pretty much ignores the fire preventers.

The awards and kudos go to the saleswoman who drives two hours in her own car, on her own time, to return a lost credit card to a customer at the airport as he's about to board a plane for Europe . . . or the engineer from another division who is parachuted in to rejigger a faulty new pump model . . . or the team in Finance that spends the weekend meeting the deadline for the annual report. Most managers don't even think about, much less praise, those who keep crises from happening in the first place.

Year after year, while proclaiming our commitment to quality, we go on devising flawed processes and turning out flawed products and services that require the services of firefighters. We refuse to take the steps needed to prevent those fires—by instilling the quality mission in our corporate culture, in our product design, and in our operations.

The LEO approach is intended to make those steps happen. LEO enables a company to truly commit to and achieve an unprecedented level of quality throughout the organization. At the same time, LEO can be applied to the solution of immediate problems, thereby fulfilling both functions—firefighter and fire preventer. Here's a case study that shows in some detail how LEO works.

> **LEO enables a company to truly commit to and achieve an unprecedented level of quality throughout the organization.**

A HELPING HAND

All across the world, it seems, nature is on a rampage. Earthquakes, tsunamis, and tornadoes have been creating havoc. When the rubble is cleared away, many residents are determined to return and rebuild. We have worked with a foundation that helps make that happen.

When we first volunteered to help this foundation in May of 2009, we explained that we would be using our LEO system and asked to take on the organization's most difficult management problem. The most pressing need, we were told, was to find ways to improve the way the foundation gathered data on all of its activities.

I remember arriving at the foundation's headquarters that August, just as the weather bureau was issuing storm warnings. It didn't seem to be a good omen. On a tour of the most hard-hit area, I was shown hundreds of concrete slabs—all that remained of the old homes. I also saw the dozen or so new homes that the foundation had put up—a disappointing number, since it was so far short of its goal of 250. We were determined to help speed up the pace.

Listen

The foundation's headquarters is on the fourth floor of a non-descript building. There was a staff of about 25 people. We had been through eight days of working sessions with the team members by satellite from our headquarters outside Detroit. Now we were to spend five days with them.

After some hours of face-to-face talk with the CEO and his top aide, digging into the processes involved in the rebuilding, we were able to create a high-level process map of the foundation consisting of just five boxes:

1. Get the money to pay for property, construction, and the like.

2. Acquire lots to build on.

3. Help potential homeowners arrange for financial and other preownership requirements.

4. Build the homes.

5. Help owners get settled.

With the foundation staff members, we analyzed each box, asking detailed questions to determine how well the processes were working and looking for bottlenecks. Yes, they said, there was enough money to achieve a faster building pace. Most of the processes in the other boxes were humming along. But when we began looking into the lot-acquisition box, a familiar bell went off in our heads.

In so many companies, the leaders dedicate themselves to collecting data associated with a problem without asking "why" and "how" questions about the process behind those data. Then they deploy one or another time-consuming, costly management tool in an effort to solve the problem.

> **In so many companies, the leaders dedicate themselves to collecting data associated with a problem without asking "why" and "how" questions about the process behind those data.**

When you complain to your doctor that you're always tired and you're not getting enough sleep, he doesn't simply write out a prescription for a strong sleeping pill—at least, not if he's a good doctor. He asks you what's been going on in your life. He wants to know whether you've been watching too many late-night movies or if you're having trouble on the domestic front. In other words, he goes beyond the symptoms and looks for the causes by asking probing questions.

In the course of our study of the foundation's "acquire lots" box, we uncovered the bottleneck. The problem was centered in two subprocesses: "identify potential lots for purchase within the target area" and "find out whether a purchase is in fact feasible." The processes were fairly complex. Ownership had to be determined and the owners found—no small matter given the exodus following the disaster. The zoning stats had to be checked, along with any mortgages, taxes due, or other liens on the property. The physical condition of the lot and the desirability of its location had to be looked into. Owners had to be interviewed to find out whether they wanted to live on the lot with a new home, wanted to sell the property to the foundation, or simply had no interest in the whole project.

Three staff members had been assigned to these tasks, but they were clearing only three lots a month for closings and construction. The reason had nothing to do with them personally—all three were hardworking people who were committed to the foundation's goals. But they were, in effect, focused on the RPM gauge instead of the MPH. Their wheels were turning, but the car was barely moving.

Each of the three had invented his own particular approach to the same task. They started the process at different stages, went about gathering data in different ways, and used different record-keeping techniques. On any given day, they might decide to alter their usual sequence of tasks, or they might forget where they had left off in the sequence and have to start again from scratch.

The confusion extended to their interactions with management. They would sometimes have to break off negotiations with the owner of a lot to check with the CEO as to whether the company was willing to meet the owner's price. There were occasions when the CEO would approve a purchase, relying on the staffers' "clean bill of health," only to learn much later, after money had changed hands, that there were liens on the property.

Enrich

With full knowledge of the situation on the ground, we had the basis for developing a solution. We made a list of all the tasks in the "acquire lots" box. Then we sat down with the CEO and three of his aides and gradually, over hours, tried to put all of those tasks into a logical, step-by-step sequence. There was debate within the room, occasionally heated, over many items, but when the working session was over, all parties were pleased with the result.

The sequence became the basis for developing a new standard operating procedure for the "acquire lots" process. Guidelines were formed for how each step of the process was to be handled.

A worksheet would enable staffers to know where they were in the process at any given time, and it also provided a record of the staffers' actions at each step of the way. Every contact with a landowner and every call to a source was to be written down and logged. Standard forms for eliciting data from some sources (government agencies, for example) were to be developed. A phone script would ensure that all the essential points were covered and the correct wording was used. New, more efficient tools and information sources would be found and made part of the process. When a particular owner proved hard to locate, for instance, skip-trace organizations would be called in.

There was one major change: the CEO would set a dollar limit on how much the foundation was willing to pay for a property—including not just the selling price but also the cost of meeting any outstanding attachments on the property—and staffers working the "acquire lots" box would no longer have to bother him every time a financial question arose during a negotiation with an owner. The limit could be updated when needed.

Optimize

Once the various elements of the solution had been identified, they were subjected to a rigorous examination to make sure the process would continue to function under unexpected but not impossible circumstances—a power failure, for example. The goal, after all, was not just to put out a fire but also to prevent it from happening again.

A schedule was established for putting all the pieces in place. Staff people were assigned to handle most of the tasks, from writing the phone script to preparing standard request-for-data forms.

The goal was not just to put out a fire but also to prevent it from happening again.

Once the blanks on the worksheet were filled in, the redesigned process was extensively tested and the results measured. Some adjustments were made. For instance, estimated times had been established for how long it would take staffers to accomplish each of the tasks within the process. Those numbers proved to be too high in some cases, too low in others.

In short order, though, it became clear that the changes had transformed the "acquire lots" function. The previous confusions and errors had been eliminated, and the time required to complete the process was drastically reduced. It used to take each of the three staffers devoted to the process a month to declare a single lot "feasible to acquire." Today, one person using the worksheet can routinely declare 15 to 20 lots a month "feasible to acquire."

FIRE, FLOW, AND FUTURE

In designing LEO, we selected three general areas of corporate activity where potential quality resides and where the Listen, Enrich, and Optimize functions could be most effectively applied. The three areas are Fire, Flow, and Future. *Fire* refers to a specific, often sudden problem in any area of the organization. *Flow* speaks to the operations side of the company. And *Future* covers new products and services.

As you will see in the following chapters, the manner in which LEO is used to tackle these three areas varies depending upon the particular circumstances. The solution is designed to fit the problem, taking into consideration the strengths and weaknesses of the organization and the goals of its leaders.

Fire

The causes of a problem may be obvious, or they may have to be ferreted out; they may be minor, or they may be so big and complex that they have to be brought down to a fixable size—for example, a drought-resistant seed versus world hunger. But before any fire can be put out, you have to know a great deal about the company and the underlying cause or causes of the problem. You start with Listen: Observe and Understand, interviewing the employees closest to the problem as well as their supervisors. You would then normally enter the Enrich: Explore and Discover phase, devising possible solutions based upon the suggestions of frontline people and managers, and also customers and suppliers, where appropriate.

Before any fire can be put out, you have to know a great deal about the company and the underlying cause or causes of the problem.

Depending upon the degree of LEO deployment, you would then move on to the Optimize: Improve and Perfect phase, which focuses on steps to avert a recurrence of the problem. The extent to which LEO is used to prevent fires instead of simply dousing them is up to the organization's leadership.

Sometimes the Listen stage is all that's needed to put out a fire.

We were called in by the president of a division of an aluminum company that was producing big rolls of sheet metal, up to six feet in diameter, and shipping them to distributors. Each truckload carried different grades of the metal banded to pallets.

The distributors were complaining. The men driving the forklifts that offloaded the pallets said that they couldn't see the labels on the rolls without getting down off their vehicles. They had to know what was on the pallets in order to deliver the rolls to the right spot in the warehouse. At one point, the president received so many gripes that even though money was tight, he spent $50,000 on new, easy-to-read labels, yet this failed to stop the grousing. The president was fuming. "I could read that label from 20 feet away," he declared, "and my eyes aren't even very good. I think the drivers just like to complain."

In the course of working with the company on a variety of other issues, we urged the leadership to Listen to its stakeholders by observing their operations. That idea worked its way down to a frontline employee who was aware of the forklift drivers' concerns. She suggested that someone should go to the scene, and the president agreed. She flew to the nearest warehouse, where she discovered that no one had any trouble reading either the old labels or the new ones from the ground. The problem: the way the rolls were being placed onto pallets and into the trucks, the labels were turned 90 degrees away from the forklift drivers on their high perch. The solution was simple: change the labeling process to ensure that the labels were always in a position where the forklift drivers could see them.

Flow

The operational side of any organization always reminds me of a river, with the various processes flowing into one another, starting with raw materials at the river's head and ending with finished products emerging at the mouth. Of course, no river runs perfectly straight and smooth—there are always some twists and turns and occasional rocks and beaver dams to interrupt the flow. By the same token, no company's operations ever achieve perfection. Total quality is always going to be a goal rather than a reality.

With some companies, all you have to do is walk into the place and you know the work flow is fine. It's like watching a top football team on game day—you can see the communication among the team members, the adjustments made to counteract the opponent's formation, and the smooth execution of the plays. Then you can walk into a company right down the street and sense the opposite. There's a herky-jerky aspect to the operation. Workers hesitate as they move from one station to another; you see expressions of confusion or concern on their faces.

No company's operations ever achieve perfection. Total quality is always going to be a goal rather than a reality.

Of course, many operational problems are not visible on the surface. That was the case when we visited a big midwestern hospital that had asked for help. There had been an unacceptably large number of no-shows and last-minute cancellations of medical tests over a considerable period of time. In some cases, patients were not receiving tests that they needed. Hospital schedules were being disrupted, and fees were being lost. Management suspected that a big part of the cause was the failure of patients to obtain their insurance companies' approval of the testing in advance.

That was not the case. The Listen phase of LEO, consisting mainly of telephone calls to the patients themselves, found that many of them had simply forgotten about the testing appointment. Others didn't know which of the hospital's many buildings they were supposed to go to. Others managed to remember the appointment and find the right building, but they had failed to follow pre-testing instructions—what foods to eat or medications to take. The insurance issue was of minimal importance.

Clearly, the patient-preparation process was broken. Moving into the Enrich phase of LEO, we looked for solutions by talking with all affected parties, including both hospital staff and patients. We also looked at best practice programs at other hospitals. In the Optimize phase, two approaches were selected: patients would be mailed a brochure that contained a map of the hospital along with instructions for preparing for their particular test; they would also receive, the day before the test, a telephone reminder of their appointment and the preparations that they needed to make. Each approach was carefully designed and redesigned to meet any contingency and then selectively tested.

Once the new process was up and running, it trimmed test cancellations by more than 50 percent.

Future

For organizations as for people, any effort to hold on to the present—to maintain the status quo indefinitely—is a waste of energy and resources. Change is hardwired into our personal lives, and we have a choice of adapting to it or suffering the consequences. As General Eric Shinseki, the former U.S. Army chief of staff, put it, "If you don't like change, you're going to like irrelevance even less."

There are essentially two ways in which companies need to prepare themselves for the kind of rapid-fire change that characterizes the modern marketplace. They need to build flexibility into their organizations, and they need to constantly improve their products and services. The shelf life of goods and ideas today is so short that we all have to, in effect, live in the future.

From a LEO vantage point, the future represents an opportunity to build greater quality into the innovation process. The Listen, Enrich, and Optimize approach can yield major benefits in developing a new product or improving an existing one.

For example, a particleboard manufacturer was getting complaints from its furniture company customers: the desks and tables made from its boards were breaking under heavy loads. The boards consisted of a core and two outer layers plus a thin finish of oak or some other wood on the outside. Resin was used to strengthen the boards, with most of the coarser, stronger particles of resin being in the core layer.

> **The future represents an opportunity to build greater quality into the innovation process.**

In the Listen phase, we gathered data from both the furniture companies and their consumer customers to understand how the boards were actually being used out in the world. Some end customers were sitting on the desks instead of just writing on them.

As part of the Enrich phase, we analyzed the sturdiness of different combinations of elements in the manufacture—more or less resin, larger or smaller particles in the boards, more or less heat or pressure.

Once we identified the settings that were most important to the manufacturing operation, we entered the Optimize phase. We used a technique that focused on improving the design of the manufacturing process. In the end, the strength of the boards was greatly increased—and their manufacturing cost was actually reduced.

GETTING DOWN TO BRASS TACKS

Up to this point in the book, I have tried to introduce you to the basic aspects of LEO—the theory and practice of this method. I have avoided the real nitty-gritty, the step-by-step details that are at the heart of any project. In the three chapters that follow, you will find yourselves in the trenches with LEO:

- Chapter 3: Putting out a Fire in a jelly bean factory.

- Chapter 4: Repairing the Flow in the request-for-quote process at a toymaker.

- Chapter 5: Creating a Future product at an automotive plant.

In these chapters, you will see some of the specific management techniques and tools that we routinely use in a LEO project in practice. You will, I hope, find practical insights that you can apply in your own organization. And you will definitely learn a lot about jelly beans, toy manufacturing, and car brakes.

Chapter Three

PUTTING OUT FIRES

I was meeting with the CEO of a large food manufacturer when he made fun of the lack of marketing know-how among the U.S. auto industry's leaders. "Maybe so," I said, "but I think I can prove to you that your company has the same kind of problem." I then kicked off the following exchange:

"What's your most important customer segment?"

"The boomers."

"When did you last meet with any boomers to find out what they thought about your products?"

"That's not my job. That's up to my product development and marketing people."

"You're just like those auto company leaders," I concluded. "They never see what it's like to buy a car because they get their cars for free, and you never make it your business to interact with your most important customers."

That exchange did not exactly endear me to my companion. But a week later, he called and urged me to spend two days at his company being shown around. "What's this all about?" I inquired. It seems that he had asked his top product development and marketing people whether they had been meeting with baby boomers. They had not. Like the CEO, they had all sorts of people who were supposed to be lifting the company's quality level, but they weren't personally involved.

Like the CEO, they had all sorts of people who were supposed to be lifting the company's quality level, but they weren't personally involved.

At the end of my tour, I met with the company's whole leadership team, and in that room I set up a blind taste test of one of the company's products, which sold for $2, versus a competing product that was selling for $1.75. All unknowing, the executives preferred the taste of the rival product.

That was when the CEO decided that he could definitely use our help, and that cutting costs in the chocolate and jelly bean plant was a good place to start.

THE MAKING OF A JELLY BEAN

Picture a one-story brick building from the 1930s with a small yard and a metal fence—something like that old grammar school you attended back in the day, only a lot bigger. Inside, the noise is staggering: Huge machines, half the size of semitrailers, shriek and groan under a low, 14-foot ceiling. The 45 operators who keep the production lines moving wear earplugs, for good reason. They also wear the usual food makers' uniform: white coveralls and hairnets. A mist of cornstarch fills the air, and clumps of starch crunch underfoot.

The plant never sleeps. Three shifts a day, seven days a week, the chocolate and the jelly beans roll. Chocolate makes up 75 percent of the production, but in terms of profit margins, the two are equal. In fact, the market for the company's jelly beans has so outstripped the plant's capacity that 12 percent of total production, worth $5 million, has had to be outsourced.

The Listen phase started with a survey of the chocolate and jelly bean operations to sort out problems and identify the most costly fire. After looking over the data and talking with management, we focused on the jelly bean operation. Not that fires were lacking on the chocolate side, but they paled in comparison to the opportunities in jelly beans.

From conversations with management and frontline people, we learned about three main problem areas in jelly bean production:

1. Too much waste scrap

2. Insufficient output

3. Overweight packages

When we compared the financial data for the three areas, our optimum target became obvious. Trimming the weight of the packages could save $1 million a year, while solving the other two issues could yield a total of only $400,000.

The package opportunity, however, had some complications. According to government regulations, bags labeled 3.5 ounces are expected to weigh at least that amount, on average, and no individual bag is allowed to weigh less than 3.2 ounces. The rule recognizes that the manufacturing process is subject to occasional error and allows for a few bags that are under the required 3.5-ounce weight. That's why you will sometimes bring your box of candy bars home from Costco and find seven bars in the package rather than the promised eight. Stuff happens. Of course, if it happens too often, you're likely to stop buying those candy bars, so manufacturers work hard to prevent such variations in their products.

In the case of the jelly bean packages, the variation in the weight of the packages was so great that there was only one way that the plant manager could be certain that they would live up to the 3.5-ounce promise on the outside of the bag and not dip below the 3.2-ounce level. He made sure the bags weighed an average of 4 ounces, with some reaching 5 ounces. The potential $1 million in savings would hopefully be achieved by making it possible for the plant to bring the average weight of a package down to 3.5 ounces.

The process of making a jelly bean sounds simple enough in theory. A plastic tray moves along a conveyor belt. One of those huge machines, called a mogul, lays down a thick layer of cornstarch across the tray, and a scraper levels the layer. The mogul lowers a machine die that creates 1,000 identical little impressions, or molds, in the layer of starch. Then nozzles in the mogul fill each mold with a sweet, syrupy mix that will become the center of the jelly bean. The tray moves on to a cold room, where the centers spend 24 hours becoming solid and chewy.

After the 24-hour solidifying period, the tray is removed from the cold room, then tipped over a stainless steel grid. The jelly bean centers are captured by the grid, while the cornstarch falls through the grid and is recycled for a repeat performance. The tray goes onto a stack and is also returned to square one. The jelly bean centers end up in a contraption that looks something like a concrete mixer, where they are turned at hundreds of rotations a minute. Sugar is added to build up the beans' harder shell, and an edible wax coating gives them their shine. Then off they go to be bagged.

Somewhere along that line in the company's factory, there was a glitch that was affecting the weight of the jelly bean bags. What complicated the task of finding the glitch was the continuous, high-speed nature of the production process. There were three lines of trays, each line with its own set of moguls, each turning out a million jelly bean centers an hour—tray after tray after tray.

Continuing the Listen phase of LEO, we moved beyond the project statement—"Reduce/eliminate overweight jelly bean packages"—toward a more action-oriented definition of our goal. To that end, we stood just past the scale, watching the finished packages of jelly beans zip by at the rate of two a second, and when a particularly heavy package arrived, we would seize it. We opened a dozen of the bags, counted the number of beans in each bag, and weighed each and every bean. It was a tedious task, but the results were worth it.

Continuing the Listen phase of LEO, we moved beyond the project statement—"Reduce/eliminate overweight jelly bean packages"—toward a more action-oriented definition of our goal.

There were a variety of theories on the floor as to what caused the weight variation. That's not unusual. People who work in a plant tend to be smart about how it operates, and often their ideas turn out to be right in one way or another. The problems they list are in fact problems, but they are not typically *the* problem—the actual reason behind the issue at hand, in this case the excess package weight. Finding the root cause of a fire requires a logical, flexible, systematic approach. That's what the LEO method provides.

People who work in a plant tend to be smart about how it operates, and often their ideas turn out to be right in one way or another.

One of the favorite theories on the plant floor was that the problem lay in a malfunction of the bagging machine. The bagging machine is set up to produce packages that weigh 3.5 ounces. The packages are loaded automatically from a series of buckets, one after another, until the ideal weight is reached. What we found in the overweight bags was an inordinate number of underweight beans. Because of those lightweights, the machine was tossing an extra bucketful of beans into a substantial number of bags, pushing their weight as high as 5 ounces.

So, yes, the bagging machine was part of the problem—but it was not the root cause. What was causing the variation in the weight of the bags was the variation in the weight of a substantial number of jelly beans—specifically, there were too many underweight beans.

We could now redefine our immediate goal. It became, "Reduce/eliminate the production of underweight jelly beans." We had moved from "overweight packaging" to "underweight product." With that accomplished, we were ready to initiate the Enrich phase of LEO.

Before moving on, I'd like to clarify what I mean by "we." There are essentially two parties to a LEO project—the mentors, meaning us, and the management and employees at the site. The planning and the physical labor are performed by a team made up of the company's engineers and frontline people. For the term of the project, we are guides and partners. Without the management and employees' participation, there is no "we" and no LEO project.

FINDING A FIRE'S FLASH POINT

Uncovering the root cause of a fire has a lot in common with pinpointing the criminal in a bank robbery. You use deductive reasoning to eliminate as many of the suspects (potential root causes) as possible, narrowing the field so that you can closely examine the suspects that remain. It's much more efficient than starting out with a detailed investigation of a large pool of suspects.

Uncovering the root cause of a fire has a lot in common with pinpointing the criminal in a bank robbery.

To accomplish that winnowing out of suspects, a LEO fire deployment typically uses split-tree analysis, which ends up looking something like a family tree. Starting at the top with the project statement, the tree grows downward through a series of connecting lines and parallel boxes.

In the case of the jelly beans, attached below the project statement box were three side-by-side boxes labeled "sugar coating," "wax coating," and "jelly bean center." The question was, could disparities in the coatings of sugar and edible wax on the jelly bean centers account for the underweight beans, or was the problem with the manufacture of the centers themselves? Tests showed that even if those coatings were uneven, they could not account for the large degree of weight variation. The side-by-side "sugar coating" and "wax coating" boxes on the split tree could now be crossed out, leaving only the third box intact: the root cause of the underweight candy was to be found in the making of the jelly centers.

The investigation now focused on the substantial number of trays bearing underweight jelly bean centers. Where were these lighter bean centers located on a given tray—in a totally random pattern, or in one or several areas of the tray, with a random pattern within each area? To answer these questions, we used a Multi-Vari Chart, a method for displaying patterns of variation. Essentially, we looked over dozens of trays for weight variation patterns that matched the weight variations we had found earlier by tearing open all those bags of jelly beans.

Multi-Vari analysis showed that the underweight centers were being created in one particular corner of all the affected trays, representing about 150 of the 1,000 jelly centers on each tray. That result allowed us to cross out the split-tree boxes that suggested other possible locations for the underweight centers. It also meant that we could put aside any concern that the location of the under-weight centers might vary from tray to tray. Now all we had to do was find out what part of the production line was affecting the corner of so many trays.

Once more, it was a process of elimination. Was there some kind of glitch involving the dies that create the molds into which the syrup is dispensed? We found that cornstarch did sometimes accumulate between the individual dies and might occasionally produce some imperfect molds on the trays, but not in any pattern that matched the Multi-Vari results, and not on such a large scale.

Was there a problem in the dispensing of syrup? If there was a pulsation in the part of the mogul that feeds the syrup nozzles, the distribution of syrup might be interrupted, and smaller quantities might be delivered to some molds. Once again, there was no sign of such a problem—and even if it should occur, there was no way it could replicate the Multi-Vari pattern of underweight centers.

Our next move was to study the dispensing of cornstarch. That's where we hit pay dirt—twice over.

As suggested earlier, cornstarch was everywhere along the production line, in the air and underfoot. Clouds of it were produced in recycling, when operators tossed shovelfuls from 50-pound bags into storage areas on the moguls, and when the moguls dumped the cornstarch on top of the trays to provide molds for the jelly syrup.

When we studied that dumping process, we saw that the cornstarch fell only about 18 inches before hitting the tray. But the flow of the starch was disrupted by a crossbeam that was part of the mogul's structural support. Across the top of the beam was a thick deposit of starch, something like the buildup of snow on a picket fence.

37

The location of the beam matched the area of the trays where the underweight bean centers were found. We concluded that the crossbeam reduced the amount of cornstarch laid down in those areas, preventing the formation of normal molds and thus of full-weight bean centers.

Why, you may ask, didn't one of the operators ever look upward and notice the offending crossbeam? Good question. For one thing, many of the workings of the mogul are enclosed—they are hard to get at and observe. For another, the process runs so fast that the operators had their hands and heads fully occupied keeping up with it.

There was just one problem with our crossbeam solution. If it was the root cause of the underweight jelly bean centers, then why wasn't every tray that came down the production line affected? We needed a better solution—a complete root cause. As Yogi Berra so wisely observed, "It ain't over till it's over."

To check our conclusions thus far, we manually covered trays with cornstarch and put them through a small run. By doing so, we removed any effect that the crossbeam might have, and the weight variations of the jelly bean centers did in fact disappear. So the crossbeam was one element of the root cause, but clearly something else was needed—and whatever that was, it involved the delivery of cornstarch to the trays.

Two new side-by-side boxes went up on the split tree dealing with the dumping of starch from the mogul: too much starch in the trays and too little. We knew that the system could accommodate an excess of starch; it would automatically be removed by the scraper that leveled the starch in the tray. So we tested the effect of delivering a less-than-normal quantity of starch to the trays—and made a startling discovery.

In the corner of the trays where the underweight jelly bean centers appeared, the combination of less cornstarch and the cross-beam prevented the creation of proper starch molds.

As the fast-moving trays approach the syrup dispensers, they come under the eye of an operator-inspector. When he spots badly formed or missing molds, with the press of a button, he can see to it that those trays avoid the syrup stage and do not continue through the production cycle.

But the operator sometimes doesn't catch the trays with the missing molds. These faulty trays then move on to the syrup dispensers. When the syrup lands in the area of the trays where the layer of cornstarch is especially thin or nonexistent, the liquid sits directly on the surface of the trays. And after the trays go through the cold room, the syrup on their surface congeals into a thin jelly layer. For want of a better word, we called it a glob, and it stays in place all the way through to the end of the line.

It seemed at first that, like those trays, we had also reached a dead end in our search for the root cause of the underweight jelly bean centers. But we decided to follow the glob-bearing trays back to the start of the bean-making process.

We kept tabs on the trays with the sticky material in the corner as they were stacked and then returned to the start of the production line, as they were covered with starch and scraped level, as the dies moved down to create molds in the starch and the syrup dispenser filled the molds, and as the trays passed into the cold room. When they emerged from the cold room, we pulled the trays from the line and measured the weight of the jelly bean centers in that special corner. They were significantly lighter than the centers in the rest of the tray.

Eureka!

After eliminating one suspect after another, after about two weeks of mentoring and learning, we had finally identified the guilty party. It was the glob.

> **After eliminating one suspect after another, after about two weeks of mentoring and learning, we had finally identified the guilty party.**

This was how the crime went down: when the layer of starch was applied, it was thinner in the areas above the sticky stuff. As a result, the molds in those areas were shallower than normal. And when the dollop of syrup was dropped into each of those molds, the excess slopped over, leaving a jelly bean center that was smaller and lighter than normal.

So in the dance of the jelly beans, the root cause turned out to be a two-step:

1. The crossbeam plus a short supply of cornstarch in the mogul created the glob.

2. The glob produced a foreshortened mold, which led to underweight jelly bean centers and overweight jelly bean packages.

FIRE PREVENTION

Moving from the Enrich to the Optimize phase of LEO, we proposed steps that would both put out the fire and prevent its recurrence.

The company had long been aware of the need, in general, to clean its hundreds of jelly bean trays. In fact, the plant had traditionally closed down for a week each year to do just that. We suggested that the cleaning take place as soon as possible to halt the production of underweight bean centers.

But before then, we urged, management should remove the crossbeam support at the cornstarch delivery stage and develop a system to ensure that the mogul's supply of starch never went below a safe level. Once the crossbeam was replaced by four new supports in the corners of the mogul, at a cost of $25,000, we tested the new arrangement, again relying on the Multi-Vari Chart. This time, the patterns of variation seen during the days of the crossbeam were absent.

Once these changes were put in place, the benefits to the company proved to be far greater than the expected $1 million in savings. When the glob problem vanished, there was no longer any need to shut down the plant each year for cleaning, and there were no more empty trays being sent through the system by the operator-inspector. All told, the LEO deployment increased the productive capacity of the plant by a substantial 15 percent, which made it possible for the company to stop outsourcing the $5 million of production and bring it back in house.

Allowing for the Human Factor

It took a while, however, before these benefits were realized. The $25,000 expenditure for the mogul redesign had to be approved, as did a schedule for a shutdown to implement the redesign. Even after all the changes were in place, the plant manager maintained the outsourcing arrangement for two years. He said he was worried that if for some reason the changes failed to yield the expected productivity gains, and he had to go back to the outsourcing company, its management would jack up the price it charged.

The human factor is always present in a LEO deployment. When we completed the jelly bean assignment, for example, which was a substantial success by any measure, including the financial one, our mentor was taken out for dinner, fed fine food and drink, and presented with a bookstore gift certificate. But it was the employees who wanted to express their appreciation who pitched in to organize and pay for the event, not, as you might expect, the company's management.

The human factor is always present in a LEO deployment.

Every organization has its own culture and its own set of personalities. Typically, though, the person in charge of manufacturing is less than enthusiastic when we arrive on a firefighting mission. To some degree, that's because it makes him look bad: why was he unable to extinguish the fire on his own? He won't put up a roadblock, since we are there courtesy of top management, but he won't be completely supportive, either. If we ask for the services of an engineer for an hour, we might get him for 15 minutes.

Of course, it's not only ego at work. Everyone on the operating side of companies today is short of resources, which have been cut way back because of the economic crunch. Downsizing rules.

Any activity that takes workers away from their normal jobs has to be suspect. Any project that adds unpaid hours to their day is the enemy.

As people start to recognize the advantages of the LEO approach, they develop more and more enthusiasm for improving quality. They see that we're there not to show them up but to show them how to make their job easier and more productive. For a company to get the maximum from a Fire deployment, managers on every level need to open themselves to the LEO process and embrace it.

> **As people start to recognize the advantages of the LEO approach, they develop more and more enthusiasm for improving quality.**

And that's true of LEO deployments to cope with Flow and Future problems as well. In the next chapter, for example, you'll see how the LEO approach was applied to a Flow project—helping a toy manufacturer redesign a request-for-quote process that was frustrating every department from Engineering to Purchasing to Assembly and sending suppliers around the bend. A key to that deployment's success was the attitude of the person who top management assigned to work with us. He was committed to the principle of continuous improvement and to quality, and he was enthusiastic about trying out this new idea called LEO. It made all the difference.

Chapter Four

FIXING THE FLOW

There are three basic ways in which movie houses make their money: from admissions, from onscreen ads, and from their concessions. They tend to be quite efficient in the way they take our money at the ticket booth and in their presentation of loud, boring ads that we, the captive audience, have no desire to watch. But their approach to serving up popcorn and soft drinks is a disaster.

According to a Stanford University study, concession sales represent about 20 percent of movie theaters' gross revenues, but they account for about 40 percent of their profits. That's because, as we know so well, their food prices are outrageously high. As CNN reported in 2010, "Movie concession operators make a 900 percent profit margin from popcorn."*

---

* *CNNMoney Online*, "America's Biggest Rip-offs: Movie Theater Popcorn—900% Markup," February, 2010; http://money.cnn.com/galleries/2010/news/1001/gallery .americas_biggest_ripoffs/2.html.

You might expect that, given the importance of concession sales to the theaters, on the one hand, and the exorbitant prices, on the other, the theaters would make it easy and pleasant for us customers to buy our snacks. Instead, we have to wait on long lines, worrying about whether we'll get our food before the film starts, simply because the theaters put too few employees behind the service counter. And those too few employees, under too much pressure, tend to be several degrees short of polite.

In other words, the concession's work flow—the process whereby missions are accomplished—is busted. Its employees are not committed to providing high-quality customer service. The staffing arrangements leave us waiting on endless lines. The pricing policies are outrageous. Uncounted numbers of patrons refuse to play that game and either smuggle in their own refreshments or do without.

Sad to say, many companies of every size and in every industry operate flawed processes, work flows that sap the organizations' energy and profitability. Managers spend their days tearing out their hair, coping with problems of quality, cost, delivery, morale, and sometimes even safety.

A TOY FACTORY'S RFQ

Processes, of course, come in two basic varieties: manufacturing and administrative. In this chapter, LEO is applied to the quintessential administrative process—creating an RFQ (a request for quote)—at a toy factory in the Midwest. You will see how an RFQ for a model train car once made a slow, agonizing trip from one desk to another, with a dozen stops, starts, reversals, and confusions along the way. And you will see how the company, over the course of five working days, used the Listen, Enrich, and Optimize approach to redesign the work flow and hasten the RFQ on its way.

The model railcar involved is not just any old car—it's the dining car of one of the trains from the 1940s that ran from Chicago to Los Angeles. In those days, long-distance passenger trains offered luxurious accommodations, from the comforts of their Pullman sleeping cars to the elegant service and gourmet cuisine of their dining cars. The trains were magnets for the stars, from Judy Garland to Bing Crosby, Humphrey Bogart to Elizabeth Taylor. And today, although passenger trains have lost much of their glitter, their history lives on in the hearts and collections of model train fans.

This toy company was helping to keep the legend alive, although getting an RFQ for a new model of an old dining car from Product Development to potential suppliers was a long, painful process. In fact, all of the more than 360 RFQs the company generated each year experienced this difficult process.

Everyone involved was frustrated. Engineering was spending endless hours preparing and amending RFQs. Purchasing was constantly bombarded with complaints from suppliers about late, inaccurate documents. The assembly plant manager was often fuming because suppliers had failed to deliver the parts that were needed to start production. Top management knew that there was a serious problem with the RFQ work flow and that something had to be done about it. The CEO thought a LEO deployment might do the job.

RFQs meandered all around the company's offices, which were housed in a two-story steel-frame building attached to the manufacturing and assembly areas. The RFQ documents could be found stored in the computers of dozens of the 1,000 or so people occupying open cubicles—although in hardly any of the enclosed executive offices toward the brick front of the building.

A great deal of responsibility for the success or failure of a LEO Flow deployment lies with the company's manager in charge of the effort, the LEO project manager. Ideally, it will be the person who is already supervising the flawed process, although that's rare. In most companies, processes that encompass more than one department often lack a single manager. (In my view, that's a mistake. A single hand on the throttle is needed when a flow problem crops up and Purchasing says, "Not my fault," and Engineering says, "Don't look at me.") So in the end, management usually has to assign someone to take on the LEO job.

A great deal of responsibility for the success or failure of a LEO Flow deployment lies with the company's manager in charge of the effort, the LEO project manager.

In this case, the person assigned happened to be an engineer, a 35-year-old Detroit Tigers fan with a continuous-improvement mindset—under the circumstances, a most valuable asset. We went over the principles and practices of LEO with him, and then he chose a team of four people, all of them in some way involved in the RFQ process: a design engineer, a purchasing agent, an engineer from a key supplier, and an IT specialist.

Generally, LEO teams end up with this breakdown: 20 percent gung ho; 20 percent negative; 60 percent wait and see. The toy company team was no exception. (Negative, by the way, is not necessarily bad as long as the person is intelligent and willing to play ball, but as any baseball coach will tell you, one insistent malcontent can cripple a team.)

The project leader introduced the members of his team to the LEO approach, explaining the tools that they would be using—and those tools only. It is one of LEO's major strengths that it eliminates the days of unnecessary training that automatically accompany so many management systems. The team members need only learn about those techniques that are appropriate to the particular project at their particular organization. The toy company team members were now ready to enter LEO's Listen phase.

THE SLOWEST TRAIN IN TOWN

The team started with the customers, those who must be obeyed—in this instance, the suppliers, the end of the line for the RFQ work flow. Team members talked with suppliers about their needs and experience with the process. They talked with the engineers who draw up the specs and the purchasing people who pick the suppliers and work with them to adjust the RFQs.

Team members watched those assembling RFQs go about their work. They saw the documents piling up in inventory on a purchasing person's computer, and they asked why. They saw an engineer making changes to an RFQ that he had sent on to Purchasing earlier that day, and they asked why. They tracked not only the forward movement of the documents but also the reverse flow of information as problems appeared toward the front end of the process.

Above all, they tried to get a picture in their minds of how this complex process actually worked and how long it was taking for the RFQ for our dining car or any other RFQ to finally reach the suppliers who were going to bid on the project.

What they discovered shocked the team members, their leader, and the company's management, as well. From start to finish, it was taking an average of 12.7 weeks for an RFQ to complete its journey—even though the value-added time, the actual amount of work time involved, totaled just 24 hours. The confusion in the process was such that it took the company four or five days just to determine the status of an individual RFQ document.

How was that possible? How could so many people continue to take part in a process that was so broken? How could suppliers deal with it on a regular, routine basis?

A designer once told me about the trouble he was having with a bridge project. To do his drawings, he needed samples of the soil and rock from the riverbed so that he could decide where the bridge's footings should go. It had taken the contractor two months to finally drill the holes and provide the designer with borings. His work schedule was in shreds. "But I understood," he told me. "Those people were really busy."

Like most of us, he was conditioned to accept the waste of time and energy and money and live with it—accustomed to doing a workaround. People put up with a lot just to get the job done. They don't want to make a fuss, get people in trouble, or make enemies. It's better to shrug and move on and let the quality drain out of the organization.

I would like to say that the situation at the toy company was an extreme example of what's wrong with too many of our companies today, but I cannot. America can do better. We must do better.

America can do better. We must do better.

Creating a Current-State Map

The LEO team spent about two days examining the RFQ work flow, top to bottom and end to end. Finally, they gathered in a conference room that had been set aside for their labors.

A huge piece of drafting paper covered one wall, and team members were encouraged to use whatever means they were most comfortable with to record what they had learned. The paper was soon covered with Post-it Notes and stick-figure drawings. From their observations, and his own, the leader created a current-state map of the RFQ process, one of the many tools that LEO may employ to cope with work flow problems.

Here's a simplified version.

The map was made up of a series of boxes in a roughly elliptical shape. At the top center, the product development people passed the design for an item—the dining car, for example—from their box to the left toward a box where engineers developed drawings. These drawings showed the major parts of the car, from plastic chairs to wheels, and how they all fit together (they looked something like the directions you get when you buy a put-it-together-yourself piece of furniture from IKEA).

The drawings then moved down the left side of the ellipse to a box where design engineers used them to create computer files containing detailed specifications. The specs would inform suppliers of the dimensions of each part of the car—the colors in the decals, the type of plastic to be used, and the performance specs. (The model train car had to be strong enough, after all, to withstand a derailment, and maybe even more than one!)

The files then traveled to the right along the base of the ellipse to a box where a purchasing agent picked three suppliers to quote the job from an approved supplier list. He sent them copies of the RFQ and shipped the original RFQ rightward again to the next box after the suppliers, which was occupied by an engineer. This engineer was assigned to update the train car RFQ drawings and specs, based in part on input from the three competing suppliers. (The suppliers, who were interviewed individually, of course, would by now be familiar with the computer files. Among the changes they suggested was the use of a slightly different plastic for a part because it would be less expensive and easier to work with.)

In the final box in the bottom right corner of the ellipse, a purchasing agent packaged the RFQs and sent them via registered mail and e-mail up the right side of the ellipse to the suppliers. Eventually, the finished dining car would be shipped left along the top of the ellipse to the toy company's production facility.

The most telling feature of the current-state map could be found in the two sets of numbers near every box. One set indicated how many RFQs were in that operation's inventory. For any given box, there might be as many as 25 RFQs, and no box had fewer than 10. The second set showed, each step of the way, the length of time it took the train car RFQ to move between boxes. Five weeks was tops, but two weeks was typical.

Some of the reasons for those oversized inventories and huge delays also appeared on the current-state map in the form of explosions. Here's what set them off:

- By the time the train car RFQ reached the final box, the list of approved suppliers had changed, and one of the original three suppliers was off the list. Another would have to be selected, sent the RFQ, and its input solicited before the RFQ could move forward again.

- The suppliers complained that the RFQ didn't include the dimensions of the car's windows.

- A supplier input for the RFQ update turned out to be wrong.

- The original engineering group drawings were inaccurate.

Each time an error was reported, the impact was felt all the way back along the line—the hip bone's connected to the thigh bone. For example, an engineer working on the train car RFQ had to stop in midstream to fix an earlier document. By the time he returned to working on the train car document and figuring out where he had left off, a new RFQ had arrived and been added to his inventory.

The ultimate snafu would take place when the confusions along the ellipse had caused such horrendous delays in choosing a supplier and providing that company with usable specs that the chosen supplier totally missed its deadline for producing the train car parts; that, in turn, would force a change in the train company's production schedule. And so the word would go out to all the boxes: dining car production has been put off for six months. Meanwhile, the people in Product Development would be mulling some new twists to add to the car's design. Unfortunately, the changes would probably require starting over with a whole new dining car RFQ.

When the LEO project leader and his team sat back and looked at their current-state map up on the wall, they realized that the RFQ process was so complex, with so many trouble spots, that they needed to focus their efforts on some portion of the work flow. Fixing the whole thing would take a lot more time than the three remaining days at their disposal.

They didn't have to spend a long time staring at the wall, however, before the answer popped out at them. Most of the problems originated in three neighboring boxes on the RFQ ellipse: where engineers draw up the specs, where a purchasing agent chooses suppliers to bid on the job, and where engineers update drawings and specs with input from the suppliers. These three boxes also represented the lion's share of the value-added time in the RFQ process.

The target had been identified. Now all the team had to do was hit it.

THE SEARCH FOR PERFECTION

Imagine what it would be like if you went to work one morning, sat down at your desk, and everything went perfectly—no complaints, no recalls, no slip-ups, not a single problem. You would probably be bored out of your skull, but not to worry: no organization—and no process within that organization—is ever going to run perfectly.

No organization—and no process within that organization—is ever going to run perfectly.

I remember overhearing a woman and her friend talking about their children's grades at school. "I don't expect Jimmy to get 100 in every class," the woman was saying. Her friend nodded approvingly. Then the woman continued, "As long as he gets 95."

She didn't expect perfection, but she did expect that her son would never stop striving for it. And that's not so far from the underlying principle of the LEO approach. It assumes that every process could—and should—run more and more smoothly. Continuous quality improvement is the goal.

There are three basic conditions that help to explain why processes tend to run amok:

- **Unreasonable work.** You're told to complete 700 assemblies this shift when four people—a fifth of your crew—are missing and your normal production goal, fully staffed, is 650 assemblies. Or you're told you have to make the company's services best in class, but the company doesn't even measure service quality. Or you're told that you have to greet every person coming into the store as if she were your best friend, this toward the end of a double shift that you're working because a colleague caught the flu.

- **Uneven work.** You have eight meetings on Monday, two on Tuesday, none on Wednesday, six on Thursday, and seven on Friday—and that's just *this* week. There's no way you can schedule your work and get it done in 8 hours when your schedule is constantly being messed around with. So you work 12 hours, and the next day you begin to fade in the afternoon.

- **Unnecessary work.** You spend hours of every day looking for lost files on your computer system . . . or waiting until somebody else finishes using the printer . . . or waiting for a meeting to start . . . or redoing a chart that you've already redone twice. The sign of unnecessary work: everyone's always busy, but everyone's falling behind.

LEO helps companies find ways to treat these conditions on a continuing, sustainable basis. The object is not to achieve perfection, but to keep moving toward it.

I think Carl Schurz, the nineteenth-century statesman, said it as well as anyone and better than most: "Ideals are like stars; you will not succeed in touching them with your hands. But like the seafaring man on the desert of waters, you choose them as your guides, and following them you will reach your destiny."

You will not be surprised, I suspect, when I tell you that the next step after the LEO team at the toy company completed its current-state map was to imagine the ideal future state of the RFQ process. Having gained an in-depth understanding of the existing process and its problems, team members were urged by the leader to suggest what the process would be like if the flow were perfect.

"At every stage, there would be no more than one RFQ waiting in inventory," one person said. Another added, "The specs would be just right when they left the design engineers, with no wrong information and no missing information." The ideas came thick and fast: suppliers would receive complete, accurate specs and drawings in plenty of time to meet their production deadline. The whole RFQ process would take two weeks tops.

Neither the leader nor any team member expected the company to achieve that ideal state, but the leader carefully noted all the suggestions. He eventually put them together to create a written document—the benchmark against which any future improvements in the RFQ process could be measured. The team, and any subsequent LEO teams, had its True North to guide it forward. It was ready to enter the Enrich phase of the LEO approach.

FINDING THE NEW FUTURE

It was time to come up with some specific and realistic ideas for improving the operation of the RFQ process. The leader asked his team to create the next future state of the process. In general, the goal was to improve the flow by removing some of the waste, but he urged them to focus on the flow rather than on trying to erase individual examples of waste.

As you will see in other chapters, the LEO approach is especially effective at finding organic solutions to management problems. We believe that problems are most often symptoms of a disease, not its cause. There's always a temptation to look for the quick fix—to take care of the symptoms, even though the disease remains and is sure to flare up again. LEO can operate on a systemic level—by studying the overall design of the RFQ process, for example. If a basic flaw can be detected and corrected at that level, the benefits will flow through the whole process.

In their study of the ellipse, the team members had found two basic flaws. For one thing, they noticed that all RFQs, regardless of their nature, were treated as though they had the same level of complexity. But the RFQ for the dining car, for example, required dozens of precise specifications to cover details such as the tiny plastic chairs and tables and lamps, while another RFQ might simply call for an empty freight car that needed a minimum of elaborate drawings and specs.

The solution: Divide the RFQ process into two separate categories, routine and complex, with the work flow tailored to the needs of each. This division would make it possible for management to assign the more efficient purchasing and engineering people to the more complex RFQs, drastically reducing the time it took to move difficult specs along. The less efficient people would be assigned to the routine RFQs while training to bring their skills up to the higher level.

If you want to get work done quickly on a complicated project, that kind of stratification can be invaluable. Interestingly, it's seldom employed on the administrative side of companies. Somehow, office operations generally opt for the cookie-cutter approach.

Somehow, office operations generally opt for the cookie-cutter approach.

The second basic flaw in the RFQ process that the LEO team identified was the confused and sometimes antagonistic relationship between the company and its suppliers. There was nothing all that unusual about it. Companies and their suppliers are joined at the hip by the contracts between them, but they have their own separate financial interests to serve. The toy company, for instance, wanted the highest-quality dining car components ever made, while the chosen supplier wanted to maximize its profit on the job by economizing on parts or slipping the dining car project into a sudden hole in its production schedule. The toy company was not always getting the quality it wanted from its suppliers—and its suppliers were definitely not hitting their financial goals when they tried to do business with an organization that consistently bungled its RFQ process.

The solution: A redefinition of the company-supplier relationship. On complex projects like the dining car, the team proposed, the company should draw from a preferred list of just three suppliers, rather than putting the project out for bid to rotating groups of suppliers. In return for a sure sale, a preferred supplier would be expected to contribute its production insights early in the game, as the complex product was being designed.

Bumps in the Road

The team recognized that there were problems with both of its proposed initiatives. On the stratification side, finding ways to classify RFQs in terms of their complexity was a challenge, particularly since it had to be done very early in the RFQ flow if it was to be effective.

The solution: Team members studied completed RFQs and developed a written check sheet for the characteristics of a complex job—sliding doors close to a window, for example, or a decoration with multiple colors on an irregular surface. If a job had, say, five items on the check sheet, it would be placed in the complex category. As it turned out, about 45 of the company's 360 RFQs a year were complex.

In developing the stratification program, a new difficulty cropped up. The engineering managers who supervised the people in the RFQ process dug in their heels. They wanted no part of an unproven initiative that might fail and cost them, as the responsible parties, their next promotion, if not their job.

The solution: A "review without blame" program was established. At monthly management meetings to assess the new RFQ design, there would be no personal criticism of the managers, and the company's leaders were on record that the mangers' careers would not suffer if the project fizzled. The objective accepted by all parties was to find out what wasn't working, not to play the blame game.

The principle of not playing the blame game is built into the LEO system: We start from the assumption that everyone wants to do well and wants the project to succeed. If a mistake is made, it's because the person involved doesn't have the right information or because the process is flawed, and the person or the process needs adjusting. That translates into a learning opportunity or more training for the person or greater ease of use for the function. In either case, the goal is to continuously improve performance. There is no value added in the blame game.

There is no value added in the blame game.

That same conviction carried over to the LEO team's second proposal: to select a group of just three preferred suppliers for complex jobs. When you hold suppliers at arm's length, when you stick with the traditional mistrust that characterizes both parties, you don't get the benefit of the suppliers' production expertise as it might be applied to the design of your products. One of the major lessons of the Japanese lean production automotive revolution was the reliance on key suppliers as full partners. The Japanese automakers went so far as to send their engineers to work in suppliers' factories to aid suppliers in improving their own internal operational efficiency and to ensure a complete and accurate exchange of information.

There are also dangers in any close client-supplier relationship, of course. Once the toy company was committed to a single preferred supplier on a complex RFQ, it would be at the supplier's mercy. The supplier might choose to arbitrarily increase its prices, and the company, with its production schedule already locked in stone, would have to either pay or suffer the financial consequences of changing suppliers. On the other hand, the preferred suppliers themselves would worry that committing so much of their production capacity to a single company might leave them vulnerable should the company arbitrarily cancel the agreement.

The solution: For each complex RFQ, the company would provide a target price that the supplier would seek to meet, a ballpark within which to operate. And the contract between the company and the supplier would include a no-blame clause to protect the supplier. The assumption was that both parties would be committed to their mutual success in the venture. The toy company agreed that if a problem or an error arose involving the supplier, it would be jointly reviewed and mutual steps taken to prevent a repetition. In the past, under similar circumstances, the toy company management would often simply remove the supplier from its approved supplier list.

I should mention that the resolution of these potential problems did not occur at the middle-manager level. There were meetings between the toy company's vice presidents of purchasing and engineering and the owners of the preferred suppliers. Essentially, the toy company people told the suppliers, "We have to change the way we've been working, because it's eventually going to drive us both out of business." Together, the two parties redefined their relationship.

As the LEO team members developed these proposed changes to the RFQ process, particularly the categorizing of the RFQs into routine and complex, they constantly checked their ideas with the purchasing and engineering people in the boxes along the ellipse. They understood the importance of getting as much experienced input as possible before the plan was implemented.

Finally, the next future state was ready to be realized, but first the team officially standardized each step of the new RFQ flow—a key element of the LEO approach.

A century ago, workers learned their jobs by listening to and watching the people around them and by trial and error. Then Frederick Winslow Taylor appeared on the scene. He used time-and-motion studies to determine the best way to do any given job. At Bethlehem Steel, for example, he observed that each worker was using his own personal shovel to handle materials that weighed anywhere from 4 pounds to 30 pounds per shovel load. Taylor's research found that the most efficient shovel load per worker was 21 pounds. So he called for the company to provide the workers with different-sized shovels for each material—shovels that would hold approximately 21 pounds no matter what the material. That way, every shoveler would always be working at peak efficiency, neither delivering too little per shovelful nor endangering his health by delivering too much.

Once Taylor had analyzed a job, he set down the results in a written standard that the worker was told to follow. So standardization of work started out as an effort to make sure that the worker followed directions—as a means of controlling employees. Today, standards serve a different function. They are aimed not at the worker, but at the supervisor. In the modern organization, employees are given extensive training and coaching so that they basically know how to do their jobs. Standards face outward, informing managers how a process is supposed to operate and how the tasks within that process are supposed to be performed.

At the toy company, there had always been write-ups of the standards for preparing RFQs, but workers had their own individual ways of following them. Some were obeying a standard from a few years back, for example, while others might be using an updated version.

One piece of the complex RFQ for the model dining car dealt with the way in which the dining area proper was to be connected to the frame of the train, which sits on the wheels. Four mechanical clips were to be applied, as well as glue at the joints. To make these RFQ requirements more visible, the LEO team proposed that the new standards be set forth in pictures as well as words. That made it easier for supervisors passing by to determine what RFQ a person was working on. They might see a more skilled engineer engaged with a routine RFQ, for instance, and assign her elsewhere.

Having standardized the new elements of the RFQ process, the LEO team was ready to envision the next-future-state map. As indicated previously, it was split between the process for creating complex RFQs and the process for creating routine RFQs. Each process was represented by the usual horizontal, left-to-right string of boxes, leading to a single box where the RFQs were assembled to be sent to suppliers.

The routine process remained intact, just as it appeared on the current-state map. But the complex RFQ process had a significant change. The box calling for input from suppliers was plucked from its midway location and moved way back to the start of the process, where the design of the product was being worked out. Now that the new map was complete, a step toward the ideal state, the team was ready to enter the Optimize phase of the LEO approach.

With the support of top management and the blame-free backing of the engineering and purchasing managers, the RFQ workers began to implement the new arrangements. With input from the chosen supplier early in the process, the RFQs were designated as either routine or complex and routed to their appropriate line of boxes. It was the fifth and final day of the LEO event.

Once the new system was actually operating, some glitches appeared. That will happen no matter how carefully you check and double-check a reconfigured process flow—and the toy company LEO team had been extremely careful. Some of the workers had trouble following the classification directions, and some of the classification decisions were inaccurate. The problems were corrected, and with that, the optimization phase of LEO was completed.

GETTING IT DONE

The results of the LEO team's efforts were striking. The pre-LEO RFQ process had a lead time of 12.7 weeks. Within three weeks after the LEO event, the lead time for complex RFQs was down to 9 weeks, and that for routine RFQs was down to 4.5 weeks. The delays and confusions that had so frustrated both the company and its suppliers were hugely reduced.

The toy company's leadership was impressed, and it immediately initiated a second LEO event to deal with some inventory problems. It was a fairly typical sequence. Companies generally try the LEO approach on a limited basis, expanding its use as they see the results. And when that happens, the new LEO events inevitably flow more smoothly and achieve even greater gains, because everyone in the organization has seen that the LEO approach actually works and is now ready to commit to the process.

Results are what count for everyone involved—especially process managers and LEO team members. When a LEO project gets under way, the managers who are directly affected will often provide just grudging support—enough to keep the team leader from complaining to management. As mentioned earlier, the team members will probably include at least one really reluctant participant. In the case of the toy company and the RFQ issues, the doubter was an IT specialist.

Results are what count for everyone involved— especially process managers and LEO team members.

There are all sorts of reasons why employees may be less than enthusiastic about any change project. One big one is: they're good at what they're doing, and they know they're not going to be as good at this new way of doing their job, at least to start with. In any LEO project, management is urged to give these employees some slack until they have a chance to master the changes—and to be sure to let the employees know that they are going to be given some slack.

The IT specialist was negative about the project, in part, because IT had come in for some earlier blame for the poor performance of the RFQ process. In my experience, IT is often managers' favorite scapegoat. In any event, it wasn't until the fourth day of the LEO event that the IT specialist was ready to fully commit herself. Then she proceeded to come up with one great idea after another. She had to see some results first.

Flow Thinking

For the IT specialist and the toy company in general, the LEO event was an introduction to a new way of thinking about processes. I call it *flow thinking*. The first question LEO asks of a process is whether it operates in such a way as to benefit the customer. Are the employees who are part of the process alert to possible pitfalls and to any chance to improve its operation? Or do they spend their days automatically moving things from inbox to outbox without further thought? At the toy company, the LEO team helped the employees handling the RFQ process greatly improve the experience of the suppliers, the customers of the process. And flow thinking led the company to change its mindset toward the suppliers, transforming that relationship from adversarial to partnership.

No company achieves flow thinking in all of its processes. Back in Chapter 1, I complained about Amazon's failure to include an audio CD in a shipment of items that I had purchased. But the same company has a return process that is a model of flow thinking: fill out a simple form, stick a label on the box, and mail. No questions asked, and the choice of another product or a refund.

No company achieves flow thinking in all of its processes

When you look at a process as a whole, you can easily see whether the flow is smooth or rough. You don't have to spend a lot of time flying Southwest Airlines to know that it's committed to flow thinking. Its processes are pointed not toward instantly making a buck, but rather toward pleasing the customer as a means of making a buck—that ancient bit of business wisdom that is so often honored in the breach. It only makes sense: companies need to examine each of their processes in terms of its overall flow and customer benefit. That way lies quality.

Companies need to examine each of their processes in terms of its overall flow and customer benefit. That way lies quality.

FLEXIBILITY IS KEY

In this chapter, I have described LEO's impact on a particular administrative Flow process, but the description doesn't begin to encompass the many strategies and tools that the LEO approach can and does apply to cope with all sorts of Flow problems in all sorts of companies. Strategies and tools are chosen to fit the particular problem and the particular company. That flexibility and the ability to tailor solutions to the situation on the ground are at LEO's core.

In the next chapter, we move to a detailed case history of LEO at work on a company's Future—aiding an automaker that is in the throes of designing a new five-passenger sedan.

COMMANDING
THE FUTURE

On a sun-filled September weekend, a dozen product development engineers set out on an unlikely mission. They were to spend the two days interviewing and riding around with local car owners at a shopping center in Oakbrook, Illinois, a suburb of Chicago. Over the next month, two more groups of engineers from the same organization undertook a similar assignment in San Diego, California, and Birmingham, Alabama. Their company was in the early stages of planning for a new midsize, five-passenger sedan, and the engineers had been assigned to find out what potential customers actually thought about, and how they experienced, their cars.

All weekend long, two-person teams in Oakbrook interviewed and drove with the car owners. They made copious notes about every detail of the encounters—not just what was said, but how the owners interacted with their cars. When an owner frowned as he stopped at a red light, an explanation was sought. "It's a small thing," the owner said, "but I just had my brakes serviced, and I still get that squeal when I come to a full stop." The complaint was carefully noted.

This assignment was not something that the engineers had done before. In fact, that was the point of the exercise. It addressed a serious, seldom-asked question: how can engineers design a new product that truly speaks to the needs and wants of customers without a firsthand understanding of those needs and wants? The question had not been considered through all the earlier generations of the company's vehicles.

The shopping-center encounters signaled the start of the Listen phase of a LEO Future deployment. After gathering the information, the company proceeded over the next 18 months to apply the LEO philosophy and tools to the development of a new passenger car that has since won major critical acclaim. In this chapter, we set forth the history of that deployment, focusing on that most essential piece of automotive equipment, the brake.

WHAT ENGINEERS DON'T KNOW

During LEO Future projects, companies develop new products or services or improve existing ones. The Listen, Enrich, and Optimize stages are all pursued, with greater or lesser emphasis on one or another, depending upon the project and the organization. But the tools and methods of Future tend to be different from those used in Fire and Flow projects. Though the ultimate goal of Fire and Flow projects is to provide value to the customer, they primarily involve internal stakeholders—they are concerned with the processes that deliver existing products. Future projects require a different, more forward-looking mindset and a direct, structured connection with those external stakeholders called "customers."

> **Future projects require a different, more forward-looking mindset and a direct, structured connection with those external stakeholders called "customers."**

There's one thing that Future deployments are not: they are not an effort to replace an organization's design and development operations. The goal here was to increase design and development quality for a given product while lowering costs; it left the organization's strengths in place.

The weekend Listen project in which car owners were interviewed was one of the unique elements of a LEO Future deployment, and for the auto engineers who took part, their customer encounters were eye-openers. One man walked away from an interview muttering, "For the first time, I understand what it means when these people talk about wanting a good-handling car." He happened to be a race-car driver on his days off. Another engineer watched open-mouthed as a housewife struggled to turn a knob in her car that would let her adjust her power side mirrors. He himself had no trouble at all turning the knob.

One of the key goals of the interviews was to inspire the engineers to become advocates for the customer within the product development process. Too often, when management calls for saving money by cutting corners on comfort or ease of use, there is nobody in product development who will stand up for the customer. The Listen project was aimed at filling that gap, making the development people far more customer-centric.

The weekend interviews required extensive preparations. Before the teams could be dispatched, they had to be trained to ask open-ended, probing questions and to observe the car owners' behavior carefully. How owners used their cars was more important, in some ways, than what they said. There are so many small problems or inconveniences that owners experience but never think to mention when a market researcher asks. They have to be seen or heard in person.

In San Diego, one team watched a woman in a shopping center wheeling a stroller that held a young child and bags of groceries. Upon reaching her car, she removed the groceries, lifted up her child, collapsed the stroller, and opened the trunk. Still holding her child, she put the groceries away and went to close the trunk. The back of the car was facing traffic, so she started pushing the trunk closed from the side of the car. She had a terrible time. Until that moment, the interview team and the company's whole development organization had assumed that trunks would always be shut from the center, from behind the car.

It is by means of such small insights that competitive advantage is gained. The trunk was eventually reconfigured to make it easy to close no matter where the owner pushes on it. As one of the car company's vice presidents put it, "You don't have to worry about big problems—you're going to hear about them for sure. It's the little ones that you often don't 'hear' that can make or break you."

You don't have to worry about big problems—you're going to hear about them for sure. It's the little ones that you often don't "hear" that can make or break you.

The engineers' interviews were painstakingly choreographed. They were to last no more than two hours. That was broken down into segments: 15 minutes talking about how the owners experienced their car; 15 minutes sitting in and walking around the car, discussing in detail how the owner used its various features; 30 minutes as passengers driving around with the owner; 15 minutes parking the car and discussing the drive and the parking with the owner; and 15 minutes wrapping up the interview.

To make sure the engineers had a cross section of people to interview who were owners of relatively new midsize sedans, an outside firm was hired to select likely candidates and arrange for them to show up at the shopping center at an appointed hour. They were paid $200 for their time.

By all accounts, the owners enjoyed the experience, and so did the engineers. The engineers had never realized, for example, how little many drivers know about the operation of their vehicles. They absorbed that lesson when they asked one driver to open the hood of his car—and he didn't know how to do it.

There were owners who simply could not figure out how to turn on their radio, as they were lost in the displays on the electronic screen in the dashboard. There were women who complained that they had nowhere to put their purse if someone was sitting next to them, short of tossing it into the back seat. Each observation and complaint was noted.

Market research had defined the new car in terms of the demographics of the target customer and the price points. Now it was up to the engineers to turn that vision into reality.

ORGANIZING THE CUSTOMER'S VOICE

Back at the company's engineering center, a sprawling glass-and-steel structure, the design team, 20 strong, started coping with the hundreds upon hundreds of comments and observations that they had collected. Their strategy, a standard Listen approach, required them to translate their notes into simple, direct statements in layman's language, the language of a customer, on individual cards. "I want quiet brakes after they're serviced," for example, became "quiet brakes after service."

In the LEO project room, a big windowless space filled with tables and chairs, anchored by an industrial carpet bearing a decade's worth of coffee stains, the team spread the cards across a group of adjacent tables. Over the next two days, with little or no conversation, the team members gradually and carefully sorted the cards into groups, piling similar-topic cards atop each other. Over here, there was a pile of cards about air-conditioning. Over there, there was a pile about windshield wipers. They then composed the words to be printed on a separate card to serve as the header card for each group. Once again, the language had to be simple, summing up the customer intent reflected in the pile of cards. "Quiet brakes after service" became part of a pile headed "quiet brakes." These headers would point the designers toward those parts of the new car that represented a chance to gain a competitive advantage over the company's other five-passenger-sedan rivals.

Though this sorting of the cards might seem like an obvious approach, it seemed a strange and probably useless exercise to many of the team members. As engineers, they were experts in everything to do with cars, and they were accustomed to setting the categories themselves and fitting any items that they found into those categories. They knew a great deal more about such matters than any customer. In effect, LEO was saying to them, "Yes, you're much smarter about cars. But we're making them to fit the customers' needs and desires, not yours."

> **In effect, LEO was saying to them, "Yes, you're much smarter about cars. But we're making them to fit the customers' needs and desires, not yours."**

Through a series of similar sortings, the new-sedan team selected the areas of the car that might yield a leg up over the competition—the electronic screen in the dashboard, for example, or the closing mechanism of the car trunk. The brake engineers found themselves confronted with some 15 individual statements reflecting customers' comments or behavior. They couldn't possibly respond to all of them; they needed to pick and choose. The engineers focusing on other parts of the car faced the same challenge.

There were seven brake people working on the new sedan, led by the brake supervisor in the chassis department. He had gone on two of the shopping-center trips. A very tall, calm, and informal engineer in his mid-fifties, he loved brakes—so much so that he had turned down chances for promotion over the years. His loyal team had developed the habit of dropping by his office each morning, coffee in hand, to chat about the day ahead.

To find the customer voices that could best guide them to a better new car, the team members sought more help from the experts—the customers. Four out of every five of those queried were the original shopping-center customers, and the rest were nontechnical employees of the company. They were all asked their opinion as to the importance of each of the 15 customer comments with regard to the brakes, giving them a priority rating of strong, medium, or weak.

Beyond that, each of the customer surrogates agreed to take a test drive of the company's car and of its chief rival. They were encouraged to experience as many of the 15 brake-related items as possible, and all through their drives, a member of the brake engineering team was present—not saying a word, but practicing passive LEO Listening. The drivers were then asked to rate the two cars on each of those 15 customer voices on a scale from 1 to 5, with 5 representing close to perfect satisfaction of the customers' needs.

Finally, a chart was created on which both sets of ratings were entered next to each of the 15 items. The chart also included, for each item, a translation of the customers' voice into technical or company language. "Quiet brakes," for instance, became, "Brake noise must be less than 40 decibels."

The members of the brake team gathered the next morning to confront the most important single decision of the Listen phase.

Their goal: to select the 3 or 4 of the 15 customer voices that they would respond to—the elements of the car's brake assembly that they would seek to improve.

Team members ranged in age from the late twenties to the early fifties, a somewhat older group than in years past. The downsizing of the auto industry had squeezed out many of the younger new hires. There was little about the scene that matched the stereotype of a business meeting—the engineers wore sport shirts and khakis, and the atmosphere was informal and down-to-earth. They simply wanted to move ahead on a responsibility that left them feeling somewhat uncomfortable. The engineering mindset is to fix things, and they would have preferred to find solutions for all of the customers' concerns. They understood that this was impractical, but that didn't mean they had to like it.

For each of the 15 customer voices, the team could see on the chart how customers rated its importance in general and whether they thought the item was better covered by the company's car or by the rival car. As they scanned the chart, the team members were particularly looking for a leapfrog opportunity— a customer need that neither the competitor's car nor their own car was really meeting. It probably wouldn't be anything very major. Brake safety, for example, is a matter of corporate conscience and federal law, so carmakers don't compete all that much on basic brake function.

Eventually, the team came up with four brake-oriented projects to focus most of their efforts on. In each case, customers had given the item the highest priority rating among the 15 items. In two of the four projects chosen, the company's car received a better score than the competition, but both scores were on the low side. The company car was behind the other car in the third project, and in the fourth, the two cars were even, with both receiving a low score of 2 on the customer voice called "quiet brakes."

With the selection of the four targets, the team was saying to the company's management, "Whatever other improvements we may or may not make to the new car's brakes, we guarantee that these four are going to happen. You can take that to the bank." The development of the vehicle, so critical to the company's prospects and involving thousands of workers and many millions of dollars, would rely upon the successful and timely completion of these four brake projects and all the dozens of projects like them that had grown out of the LEO customer interviews.

Toward a Better Design

The brake supervisor and his team, now down to five members, entered the Enrich phase of the LEO deployment, dedicated to finding the best designs for meeting the four critical brake targets. The supervisor began by putting the team members, who had been working on all sorts of assignments involving all sorts of brakes before the new project, through an intensive program of study to familiarize them with the brake system on the company's existing sedan.

With that information under their belts, they undertook a detailed comparison of the design elements of the current brake with those of six other types of brake. The goal was not to choose the best design among them but to inspire the engineers to come up with new, more creative design approaches. They would spend two weeks at this task, exploring the strengths and weaknesses of the various models.

The goal was not to choose the best design among them but to inspire the engineers to come up with new, more creative design approaches.

The technique used was a Pugh matrix, named after its Scottish creator, Stuart Pugh. After earning a degree in mechanical engineering from London University, Pugh worked in the aviation and electronics fields, quickly rising to the post of chief designer. In 1970, though, at the not-so-ripe age of 41, he turned his back on industry, became an academic, and gradually developed his groundbreaking design theories. His matrix provided a holistic view of a company's needs and the alternatives available to it. One of its major advantages, Pugh wrote, is that "as the reasoning proceeds and a reduction in the number of concepts comes about for rational reasons, new concepts are generated."*

To create the Pugh matrix, the brake supervisor lined up images of seven brake types across a wall of the project room, starting with the company's current disc model. The others were a drum brake, two regenerative brakes, and three disc brake variations.

To the left of the images was a vertical column of 15 criteria by which the engineers would judge the various brake designs. The criteria included a handful of customer voice items, "quiet brakes" among them, but the majority of the criteria represented company requirements, such as "low initial cost" and "low maintenance." Using the 15 criteria, the engineers proceeded to rate all of the

---

* Stuart Pugh, *Total Design: Integrated Methods for Successful Product Engineering*. Boston: Addison-Wesley, 1991, p. 74.

other brake types on whether they were better than, worse than, or the same as the brake on the company's current sedan.

They combined and recombined the components of the various brake styles, analyzing the results and searching for a new design concept. They discovered, for example, that on only one count, low initial cost, was the drum brake superior to the sedan's brake; the same was true of the two regenerative brakes, but they were better on a different criterion, low brake drag.

By the end of the second week, the team members had succeeded beyond their own expectations, creating an entirely new brake design. That was the good news. The bad news: because it would take so many months to fully develop, the new design couldn't be used on the current project and would have to be put aside for the time being. The engineers had also come up with some improvements on the existing disc brake design, although not enough to achieve their goals for all four of the critical customer voices.

Then the youngest and least senior person on the team, a 29-year-old design engineer, offered a suggestion to deal with one of the voices, "quiet brakes." His idea: "Why don't we now take the improved caliper, rotor, and pad design and see how far we can take it using Dr. Taguchi's methods?" The brake supervisor gave the idea his blessing, but made it clear that other brake improvement projects would also be pursued.

THE ENDGAME

With that approval, the improved disc brake entered the LEO Optimize phase. There it would be put through a process called *robust optimization,* which was first developed by Dr. Genichi Taguchi, a Japanese-born quality pioneer. The process is intended to give a product superior performance while at the same time lowering its cost.

The process is intended to give a product superior performance while at the same time lowering its cost.

At this point, I need to introduce you to some engineering terms. Start with *robustness,* which refers to the ability of a product to perform up to standard in spite of *noise.* Noise, in turn, is any potentially disruptive element, ranging from excess operational heat to misuse of the product by the customer to bad weather conditions.

The traditional engineering approach to optimization creates a design that meets company requirements. But when it's tested under real-life conditions, where new noise elements are introduced, the product design inevitably must be adjusted to fit. In some circles, this is known as Whack-a-Mole engineering: As soon as one problem is hammered into submission, another pops up. The process is costly and time-consuming. Dr. Taguchi insisted that the adjustment of the design for noise factors should take place before the production model is created, and he found a strange and wonderful way to do just that. It reverses the traditional order of things.

Robust optimization starts by reducing the new product's performance variability. Once the product's output is stable, the new design is adjusted to meet company and customer requirements. This two-step process is another unique aspect of a LEO Future optimization.

Now, let's get back to our young brake engineer. The "caliper, rotor, and pad" he referred to make up the core subsystem of a disc brake. The rotor is a round metal plate attached to the car wheel, and it rotates in tandem with the wheel. The caliper is a metal assembly that houses a piston. The brake pad, or lining, is attached to the piston. When you step on the brake pedal, that pressure—hard or soft—is passed on to the piston through hydraulic fluid. The piston then pushes against the rotor with its brake pad, causing the car to slow down or stop.

Boiled down to basics, that braking event consists of an input and an output, a *signal* and a *response*. The signal is the hydraulic pressure initiated by your foot on the brake pedal. The response is the braking force, or torque, applied to the rotor.

Ideally, all of that energy will be used for braking. In practice, noise factors get in the way. The brake pads wear down; the rotor gets out of alignment; the surface of the pads becomes slick with rain. The result: the car vibrates when you step on the brake, or it takes too long to stop, or the brake squeals—all the symptoms that cropped up in the interviews with car owners back in the Listen phase of the LEO deployment. The greater the number and strength of the noise factors, the further the brake moves from its ideal function. Robust optimization is a way of moving the design closer.

To make it clear how revolutionary Dr. Taguchi's ideas are, let's look at the usual approach to quality control. It applies a single measure to the products that roll down a production line: either they meet the company's standard or they don't. The inspector tosses aside those products that fall below the standard and allows the others a safe passage. Products are either black or white, approved or discarded, with no shades of gray allowed.

Yet, as we all know, the gray is there. Some of those approved products just managed to get by, whereas others passed with flying colors. The company doesn't care about the differences within the approved products, but customers do. Would you rather have a car brake that just managed to pass through quality control or one that substantially surpassed the minimum requirement?

The pass-fail mindset drives customers around the bend. Sometimes the company's products perform well, sometimes they perform very well, and sometimes they just barely manage to do their job. Customers want consistency in their products, and nowhere more than in their car brakes. They dote on reliability and despise variability.

Pretend you're a football coach for a minute—say, Mike McCarthy of the Packers or Mike Tomlin of the Steelers. You have two field goal kickers. It's early in the season, and both of them have converted on every try, a dozen each. But Kicker A has clustered every kick right down the middle of the goal posts, while Kicker B has scattered them all around, with several just managing to get through. Which player are you going to go with when the game is on the line?

No question, right? The old "good enough" standard, for a kicker or for a product or process, doesn't cut it anymore. Coaches and customers of every sort, including football fans, want and expect more. They want to reduce the spread of products around the target; they want high-level consistency. When drivers hit the brake pedal, they want the same amount of braking each and every time.

That's the goal of robust optimization, and it leads to all sorts of changes in the optimization process. In the old system, if your product lives up to the company specification, you relax. In a LEO optimization, even if the specification is met, the effort to make the product better and more cost-efficient goes forward. That no-limit mindset has a powerful psychological effect, inspiring the design crew to unleash their imaginations and sparking their enthusiasm.

> **In a LEO optimization, even if the specification is met, the effort to make the product better and more cost-efficient goes forward.**

To see robust optimization at work, let's return to the subsystem brake team, now consisting of the young engineer and just two other colleagues. Their basic task was to vary aspects of the design to observe how it performed under a variety of noise conditions. Their larger goal was to find a combination of changes in design that would reduce the effect of noise on the brake, improving performance without increasing the cost. Noise was the enemy because it shifted the energy output of the brake away from the target, increasing variability.

To see how any given set of design changes affected performance, the team would test them on a dynamometer, an instrument that would spin the brake's rotor and then measure the design's braking force. There were six of these 18-foot-long, 7-foot-high dynos, as they're familiarly known, in the basement of the engineering center. The results for each potential new design would be compared to those for the existing improved brake design.

The tests had to allow for a host of variables—so many, in fact, that not all of them could possibly get their due. The brake team whittled them down to the most important ones:

- **Noise conditions.** New designs were run under conditions of low temperature, wetness, and an 80 percent worn pad. The existing design was run at normal temperatures, dry, and with a 10 percent worn pad.

- **Control factors.** There were a total of eight items that would be used to increase the brake's output—six for pads and two for rotors. The pads could be thinned or thickened, made of different materials, or even redesigned. The rotor materials and design could be altered. For each of the eight controls, three options were tested—three different materials, for example, for the rotor.

- **Input pressure.** The various designs were subjected to four levels of brake pressure, from just a touch of one's foot on the pedal to just short of a sudden stop.

In the end, a total of 18 versions of the brake were run through a dynamometer. It took a week. Eventually, the most robust design emerged. It delivered a more consistent braking force under typical noise conditions and at a significantly lower cost.

That success ended the first stage of the LEO robust optimization. The second stage was relatively simple. Once the design was shown to be performing consistently, it was a matter of adjusting whatever braking force the design delivered in order to meet the needs of customers and the company. You don't want the braking force to be set so high, for example, that a touch on the brake pedal will send the poodle through the window. The adjustment is a kind of balancing act, with cost on one side and performance and quality on the other. But the end result is a much-improved, reduced-cost brake design.

The Power of Robust Optimization

I have more to say about the brakes end result, but I'd like to pause here for a moment to emphasize how different robust optimization is from the usual approach to improving a product or process. Consider that the most difficult of noise factors is the misuse of a product by its customers.

I'm thinking of a simple pair of scissors that is intended to cut paper and cloth. That's what the owner's manual says, and that's what the scissors do quite well. But a certain percentage of customers ignore that information and insist upon trying to use the scissors to cut leather or plastic. They don't work, and if the customer perseveres, he can ruin the scissors, not to mention what he's cutting into.

The manufacturer can plaster a warning message about the scissors' limitations across the packaging. That might help a bit, but such a negative message might also turn off many potential customers.

Or the manufacturer can simply surrender and bolster the design of the scissors so that they *will* cut leather and plastic. The working parts of the tool can be beefed up and new, stronger materials used. Of course, that's going to be expensive, so the price of the scissors is going to rise. And the higher price is going to turn off a lot of customers, especially those who don't care about having scissors that are strong enough to cut leather and plastic.

That's the usual approach. Companies look at product or process problems, real or potential; track down the cause; and try to find a fix for each of them. Aside from the cost involved, every change to improve a system can easily weaken some other element of the system, and the Whack-a-Mole game begins. Instead of focusing on failures, robust optimization focuses on the much smaller number of ways in which a company can make things go right.

Instead of focusing on failures, robust optimization focuses on the much smaller number of ways in which a company can make things go right.

In a LEO Future deployment, the scissors problem would be resolved by improving the efficiency of the original design. Reducing the tool's variability under all the relevant noise factors would lead to a product that could handle virtually any challenge, including customer misuse, without burdening it with undue costs.

Time and again, I have received calls from chief engineers of companies where a robust optimization was scheduled. The conversation follows a regular pattern:

"Subir, I don't understand what you want to do here. This way of optimization isn't how we do it. It's so different that I don't know where to begin."

"I understand, Joe. When I first talked to Dr. Taguchi and he told me about his way of optimizing, I didn't get it. Like you say, it was so different. But then I saw how it worked, in any environment. You'll see, Joe; it will work at your place, too."

In fact, that's what was happening at the auto company's engineering center. After putting their 18 model brakes through the dynamometer, the brake engineers selected the best-performing design. They predicted that, compared to the company's existing brake, it would reduce the effect of noise on braking force by 75 percent.

THE OPTIMIZED BRAKE

When a fail-safe production-level version of the new design was tested, the 75 percent reduction in the effect of noise dropped to 60 percent. But it still represented a remarkable advance. The optimized brake was substantially lighter, less expensive, and more reliable than its predecessor—and it lowered the incidence of brake squeal by a factor of 20! The "quiet brakes" critical target was achieved, in spades.

Once the chief engineer saw the optimization results, the brake's story line took a new twist. The design was so efficient, he decided, that it would allow the company to substantially reduce the size of the brake on the new sedan. That move saved the company millions of dollars.

When the young engineer presented the results of the optimization to the full group of brake engineers, the response was generally enthusiastic, but not all of his listeners were pleased. A few of the older men who had worked on the previous brake design felt that this new and improved version was putting their expert reputations at risk. In fact, the development of the improved brake had less to do with the expertise of any engineer than with the power of LEO.

From the gathering of real-time customer attitudes and experiences by engineers to the use of such tools as the Pugh matrix and robust optimization, LEO represented a significant sea change for the company. It posed questions that the company's engineers had not considered before, and it provided them with an unfamiliar approach to new product development. And as they and their management discovered, the benefits were substantial.

In this and the previous two chapters, I described LEO deployments that were focused on putting out Fires, improving operational Flow, and developing Future products. In the next three, my focus narrows, with a chapter devoted to each element of LEO—Listen, Enrich, and Optimize. In addition to a more detailed look at these elements, each of the chapters will include three case studies.

In the next chapter, for example, you'll see how the Listen phase of LEO was deployed at a lumber company, a hospital, and a pet food company. It's a mini-demonstration of the variety of venues in which LEO is comfortable and effective.

Chapter Six

LISTENING HARD

I n the spring of 2010, a complaint about the new iPhone 4 went viral. Hordes of people were finding that the strength of the device's signal was compromised—beyond the limitations of the service provider, AT&T—if they held it by its lower left corner. This was especially a problem for those who were left-handed. Finally, late in June, Apple issued an official response by Steve Jobs to his customers' problem:

> Gripping any phone will result in some attenuation of its antenna performance. . . . If you ever experience this on your iPhone 4, avoid gripping it in the lower left corner in a way that covers both sides of the black strip in the metal band, or simply use one of the many available cases.

This statement was greeted badly in many quarters. It seemed to blame the customers for their problem: they were holding the phone wrong, and/or they were too cheap to spend $30 or so for a case.

I have often marveled at the attitude that so many companies, and their leaders, display toward customers. In the iPhone instance, how difficult would it have been for the company to apologize for any inconvenience and promise to try to do better with the next model? It might not have satisfied every complainant, but it would have been a civilized, forthcoming kind of exchange. It would have demonstrated that Jobs was truly listening to his customers and responsive to their concerns.

As of this writing, Apple is still riding high on the strength of its stylish, groundbreaking devices, but competitors are closing in. There may come a time when the company finds itself more dependent upon the goodwill and loyalty of its customers and its reputation among potential customers. None of those things was bolstered by the iPhone statement.

The failure to truly listen to customers is at the heart of many a corporate failure. By the same token, careful, intelligent listening is a crucial step on the road to organizational success.

Careful, intelligent listening is a crucial step on the road to organizational success

As you have seen in earlier chapters, listening is also at the heart of LEO—it is the first phase of every LEO deployment. Up to this point in the book, I have treated listening as simply part of the LEO process. In this chapter, it is my primary focus. I suggest how best to go about it, as well as the pitfalls to avoid, and I offer three case studies of the Listen approach being applied to very different problems in very different industries and under very different circumstances.

Listening in LEO is not a rigid, step-by-step technique for finding out what customers want or need. In fact, there is no strict methodology that can possibly be successfully applied to the infinite variations of a customer's experience and desires. Each organization is unique in terms of its products and processes and the way it interacts with and is perceived by its customers.

> **Each organization is unique in terms of its products and processes and the way it interacts with and is perceived by its customers.**

So Listen is, like every aspect of LEO, eclectic—tailored to the particular company and its particular customers. And those customers may not be the folks who are buying the company's products. They may be internal customers—the people working in the call center who are making an unusual number of errors. They may be suppliers—the people who no longer answer your calls because they lose money trying to cope with your unreliable requests for bids.

So in a LEO deployment, you may be listening in order to find a new service for existing customers . . . or to improve a current product . . . or to reduce the amount of scrap and rework in your plant . . . or to deal with any of a dozen concerns that come under the heading of Fire, Flow, or Future.

Companies typically rely on marketers and customer service people to find out what customers want and don't want. The marketers conduct surveys and focus groups. They connect with customers and potential customers on company websites, on Facebook pages, and via Twitter. The customer service department records customers' comments and complaints as expressed in e-mails and phone calls. No question, the information gathered in this way is vitally important and should be part of any company's product planning.

Meanwhile, line managers are constantly monitoring their areas, whether they're in Production or Accounting, and they provide company leaders with essential information about these operations.

But when serious problems arise in the sales or operations areas, or when a new or improved product is required, these sources of information are not enough. Management needs a better comprehension of the situation, one that is both broader and more intimate—broader because the particular situation must be understood in the context of the organization as a whole, and more intimate because the best solutions emerge only from in-depth knowledge of the circumstances and the people involved.

LEO is dedicated to the proposition that the most efficient, most profitable strategy calls for the conversion of customers' needs and wishes into specific corporate goals. The Listen stage delivers the raw material for that conversion.

HOW TO GO ABOUT IT

Whether you're involved in a Fire, Flow, or Future deployment, the first order of business is to get out from behind your desk and go where the action is—where the problem is happening, or where the customers are buying and using your product. Whatever your particular travel destination, whether it's down the hall or in another state or country, the same rules of the road apply. The most important of them is that you get up close and personal. You can't really know what's going on, what customers are thinking and feeling, unless you go to the source. The second- or thirdhand reports of your aides will not suffice if you hope to make decisions based on reality.

> **You can't really know what's going on, what customers are thinking and feeling, unless you go to the source.**

The Japanese call it going to the *gemba*, "the real place." On Japanese TV, news people report "from the *gemba*," and detectives speak of a crime scene as the *gemba*. There is a lesson built into the concept that is so essential—and so often ignored by companies seeking to adopt the lean production approach pioneered by the Japanese.

When a Japanese businessman goes to the *gemba*, when he spends time on the factory floor or in the call center or talks with a customer in her home, he treats these people with respect. The worker is not simply a cog in the corporate wheel, but a real person with a brain who knows his job and can probably do it better if he is given half a chance. The customer is not simply a data-providing cipher, but a person with tastes and sensibilities who can, with a few words, change the course of a whole organization. The Japanese executive approaches people with courtesy and speaks to them politely and appreciatively.

This respect for the individual regardless of the disparity between his station in life and your own is a vital element of the LEO Listen phase. It is not just a humane and civilized way to behave—it is also effective. If you truly want to learn from workers and customers, you need to make them feel at least somewhat comfortable in your presence. Comfort breeds wholehearted cooperation, which in turn yields insights.

> **Comfort breeds wholehearted cooperation, which in turn yields insights.**

I remember accompanying an executive of a hotel chain who was interviewing a man and his wife who were guests at one of the chain's properties. The executive was tall and immaculately dressed, with the bearing of a drill sergeant in the Marines. The guests were nervous, and at first the executive didn't help much. He actually cared about his guests' attitudes toward the hotel, but he started out by firing off questions like, well, a drill sergeant. Their responses were minimal.

Then suddenly, he changed—he probably caught my unhappy expression and remembered that we had earlier discussed this whole *gemba* aspect of LEO Listen, and he eased up. He told the couple a story about a miserable stay he'd had in a hotel in London, groaning and laughing about it. He asked whether they were enjoying their visit in the town and whether they had taken a boat ride he had particularly enjoyed. In other words, he began treating them respectfully, as people instead of objects.

Once that rapport was established, the couple willingly and fully shared their reactions to the hotel. They liked the extra rolls of toilet paper and the service in general, but they complained about the rain. "We know it's not your fault," the wife said, "but we got tired of getting wet."

Her comment inspired the executive to introduce a new feature to the hotel—an inexpensive umbrella that was hooked over the rod in every closet with a note that read, "We hope the weather will be wonderful for you, but just in case." It attracted much favorable comment from guests and a spate of publicity that brought the hotel to the attention of many potential guests.

You may recall that the Listen phase of LEO also encompasses two other desired actions: Observe and Understand. In going to the *gemba*, your mission is to understand what's happening there, or not happening, as the case may be. (The problem may be one of omission, a failure to keep up with the latest best practices, say, rather than one of commission.) In addition to asking questions to advance your understanding, you need to keep your eyes open, to watch how a worker performs a task or how a customer uses her vacuum cleaner. You also need to observe how a customer reacts to your questions so that you can tailor your questions and the way you ask them to fit that individual's taste.

Once the people you are seeking out comprehend what you're looking for, let them talk without interruption, except to gain some necessary clarification. There's no sense in telling them what you think—that won't yield any valuable information. It can only confuse them and get in the way. Let them have the floor while you get out of the way. As the ancient Greek philosopher Epictetus suggested, "We have two ears and one mouth so that we can listen twice as much as we speak."

Even though you keep your comments to a minimum, you are constantly communicating with the people you interview in a variety of nonverbal ways. If you stand there with your arms folded and your foot tapping, the negative message is just as clear as if you spoke it. If you sit stiffly and you wear a stern, executive expression, like that drill sergeant of a hotel manager, you are going to make the interviewees feel uncomfortable. And if your gaze constantly wanders away from them as they speak, you're going to turn them off.

One way to demonstrate your sincere interest in people's experiences and ideas is to take notes. This also demonstrates the importance you attach to what they say and the real possibility that you will act upon their words and opinions later on. Also, if your memory is like mine, notes are simply a practical way to make sure you don't forget the details of what you're hearing.

Capturing the Full Truth

There is a potential pitfall awaiting those who embark on the Listen phase: the temptation to stop too soon. Too often I have seen leaders call a halt because they have gained several insights and are impatient to put them to work. "Enough talking," they insist. "I want to see some results."

The impulse is understandable. If you spend most of your days in meetings about what will or should be done, you can become impatient with preliminaries and eager to see some action. But as a Listener, you need to resist the impulse unless you are truly confident that you have captured the full truth of a situation. Have you talked to a large enough cross section of people, or are you basing your conclusions on a too-narrow sample? Have you spent enough time observing a production operation or customers' behavior with your product to be sure that you understand them well enough to frame a new policy or strategy?

The quality that LEO can deliver is directly proportional to the quality of the information gathered in the Listen phase of deployment. That information, gathered from internal and external customers, determines the whole course of the LEO deployment. Yes, there are all sorts of powerful tools that can be applied to work with the data collected in order to set targets and solve problems, but their outcomes are limited by the nature of the Listen input. What goes in the front end determines what comes out the back.

In its focus on an accurate reading of customers, LEO does not exempt suppliers. Even if your company is a supplier serving consumer products companies, we urge that you Listen to those companies' customers—to the end customers.

I remember clearly the description a friend gave me of his predicament. He was an engineer, working for a firm that made plastic parts for a car company. There came a time when his customer gave him an order to make something that my friend knew would be a nonstarter with the public. He tried to delicately suggest to the customer why car buyers would not appreciate the design, but he got nowhere. "We made the thing, exactly the way they wanted," my friend told me, "and it was a disaster, just the way we knew it would be. I was dying to tell them, 'I told you so,' but you know damn well I didn't."

For their own survival, suppliers need to be smart about what the end customers want, and the best way to get there is to go to the *gemba*. Many major suppliers are doing just that these days, supplementing the consumer research that their customers may be doing. In some cases, the consumer goods companies have actually turned the whole task over to their partner suppliers—a kind of ultimate outsourcing.

Whatever a company's product or process, its success will ultimately depend upon its ability to meet the needs and wants of its customers. As you will see in the case studies just ahead, LEO's Listen process is a flexible and efficient way to find out exactly what those needs and wants really are.

Whatever a company's product or process, its success will ultimately depend upon its ability to meet the needs and wants of its customers.

A LUMBER COMPANY MAKES THE GRADE

At age 35, an unassuming executive suddenly found himself in charge of an empire. It was just one piece of the vast northwestern holdings of a giant lumber company, but as regional manager, Keith, as I'll call him, was responsible for 700 workers who felled the trees, transported the logs, and operated the three sawmills in his part of Oregon.

As he soon discovered, though, there were problems. His region had far more capacity than it had sales. Keith needed to come up with some new customers or sell more to the customers he had—or both. He had little confidence that taking a few purchasing agents out to lunch would do the trick. But he had heard about LEO, and after he learned how it worked, he decided to sign on.

Like most of the company's executives, Keith had earned his stripes the hard way. He had started out in the forest, operating a skidder tractor and a chain saw, before moving on to a beginner's job in a mill. It wasn't long before he became a supervisor and eventually the youngest mill manager in the company's history.

Keith ran a safe and successful plant, and he and his family, including a wife and two young children, were comfortably settled in the mill town when the call came to move up to regional manager. He had demonstrated his business smarts, substantially increasing the mill's sales, and he was a respected leader—even though, as a devout Christian, his vocabulary differed from that of many of his lumberjacks and mill hands.

In preparation for LEO deployment, Keith called his marketing lead and three of his plant engineers into a meeting that would last the whole day. They sat around a table in a room with views out over the Cascade Range, its volcanic peaks still bearing traces of snow on this summer day. Over coffee and doughnuts, Keith laid out the problem: like a high-IQ student with a C average, the region wasn't performing up to capacity.

The four men turned their attention to a list of existing customers, gathering and analyzing the data. How much of what product did each of the customers buy? What was the dollar value of those sales and the profit margin on them? With that information in hand, Keith and his aides sat back and talked about where to seek increased sales and which customers to target. By day's end, they had their answer: window manufacturers.

The gathering and analysis of data is an important early step in any LEO Listen process. In this case, Keith and his people needed to have a clear financial picture of their customers in order to help them decide where to focus their sales efforts. But as he understood, if his team was to win more orders, it would have to become a great deal more knowledgeable about the customers' operations, and the best way to do that was to go to the *gemba*.

The gathering and analysis of data is an important early step in any LEO Listen process.

"How many of you have ever visited any of our customers' window manufacturing plants?" Keith asked his aides. None of them had. He wasn't that surprised. The company left that to the salespeople. Keith himself, along with a sales rep, had spent an hour in the offices of a window maker, negotiating a settlement with a purchasing agent, but they hadn't gotten close to the plant itself.

Keith intended to change that as part of the company's participation in LEO. He explained the Listen phase to his team as a series of logical steps:

- We have a lot of different kinds of customers in those companies. There are the guys on the receiving dock who unload our trucks, the operators who assemble and finish the windows, and the people who install the windows in homes. Last but not least, there's the homeowner who is going to have to live with the windows for years.

- The people who run the company have to be given a good reason for buying more of our lumber.

- For us to find that reason, we need to develop a much greater depth of knowledge about the way the plants operate and the problems and needs of the people who work there.

- The best way to acquire that knowledge is to interact with those people in person, to listen to them and observe them as, and where, they work.

And that's the plan Keith set in motion. He increased the team to eight people, adding a lumber grader, another marketing rep, and two mill managers. Then he contacted the largest of his window customers and explained that he and his team wanted to get a better understanding of how their lumber was being used. The customer was pleased by this obvious desire by a supplier to improve its service.

A day was set, and the night before, the team took a commuter airline flight to Rapid City, South Dakota. After dinner, Keith called the team together in the hotel and finalized their plans. Four two-person teams would watch operations in the plant and then talk to the workers. As required by the plant manager, the talks would take place during the workers' regular breaks. The team members would carefully write down what they saw and heard in the notebooks Keith had provided.

He and his team spent a total of 10 hours at the window manufacturing plant that day, and returned to Oregon the next morning. Over the next week, they learned to use some of the Listen tools I've described in earlier chapters. They translated their notes into simple, direct statements and wrote them on cards. The cards were sorted into categories, and the categories were prioritized in terms of their importance to the customer. The results were studied and analyzed. Possible solutions and initiatives were proposed and debated, and the results were discussed with window makers.

Results

As it happened, the LEO approach served Keith and his company very well—on three fronts.

First, the team had observed that some people in the window plant were having trouble with the confusing but traditional system for grading lumber. As a result, they had a hard time ordering the kind of wood they needed.

Boards may be made of hard or soft wood, and each has its own uses, although sometimes soft may be substituted for hard—in shelving, for example. (In fact, hard wood is not necessarily harder than soft wood.)

The grade given a board is based on the judgment of an individual mill hand (and is then stamped onto the board). Grades range from "Clear Face Cutting," a board that is free of knots or other defects on both sides, down to "Below Grade," a board with defects on more than 80 percent of its surface. There are five or so grades between those two, most of them referring to one side of the board.

At the window plant, employees who were looking to buy lumber to be used for, say, interior sash on a particular project would have to choose among pine, oak, maple, and a white-painted softwood, all of them of several possible grades.

Keith developed a unique grading system designed specifically for his window-maker customers. It was based on the application that a board would be used for rather than on the old system. When ordering wood for interior sash, for example, the window makers simply had to choose between "interior sash for staining" and "interior sash for painting." Keith's mills took care of the rest.

Because the right lumber was used to handle the job, the consumer end customer received a better-looking window. And the grading change doubled Keith's sales to window manufacturers.

Second, his team also observed several operations that were being performed at the window plant that could be done more efficiently at the lumber mill. For instance, when the preparation of wood for finger joints moved to the mill, it produced extra income for the mill and relieved the window customers of a troublesome process.

LEO's greatest benefit for the window makers, though, was the visiting team's recognition that in two assembly areas, the company could substitute a lower-grade, less-expensive board without damaging the functionality or appearance of the window. In other words, costs came down while quality and functionality increased, which is often counterintuitive. The cost savings were another reason why the window companies doubled the size of Keith's order book.

Costs came down while quality and functionality increased, which is often counterintuitive.

A HOSPITAL FINDS A CURE

One afternoon several years ago, the physician in charge of infectious disease control at a large community hospital was summoned to a meeting with the CEO and her staff. The physician—I'll call him Dr. Arnold—was pretty sure what the topic would be, and he was right.

An internal hospital report had just landed on his desk showing that the rate of hospital-acquired infections (HAIs) among inpatients was 10 percent higher than the average for hospitals around the state. In no uncertain terms, the CEO informed him that she wanted an explanation. She also wanted to hear his strategy for lowering that infection rate. Dr. Arnold could satisfy her on neither count. It was a stressful meeting.

The next day, his stress level rose even higher. The local newspapers got hold of the report. The headlines made the situation appear even direr than it was, and when he was called into the CEO's office that day, he expected the worst. Instead, the boss had a suggestion.

The hospital had begun introducing LEO in part of its operations, and she thought the approach might be helpful in dealing with the infection problem. She put Dr. Arnold in touch with staff people who were involved in the deployment, and he put aside time each day for a week to study the system. Meanwhile, he began to assemble a multitalented team to review and analyze the hospital's infection data. By the time he felt confident about his understanding of LEO, his team was ready; in addition to Dr. Arnold himself, it consisted of an operating room nurse, an emergency room doctor, a supervisor of inpatient care, a doctor of internal medicine, and a radiology technician.

To kick off the Listen phase, Dr. Arnold and the other members of the team gathered in a bright and comfortable conference room in a new section of the hospital, a far cry from the facilities in the 40-year-old main building. They set about examining infection statistics for the various areas of inpatient care, from cardiovascular diagnostics to pediatric surgery. The goal was to eliminate areas with little or no increase in infections so that they could pinpoint problem areas on which to focus their search for a cause.

The technique—the split-tree analysis described in Chapter 3—failed to uncover any promising leads.

Dr. Arnold next divided his group into two-person teams. They were assigned to go to the *gemba*, where the action is. Each team explored one or another part of the hospital. In radiology, for example, they watched how the technicians worked with people who were being given X rays or CT scans. They observed the precautions being followed in surgeries. They checked to make sure that nurses were cleansing their hands after working with a patient in the infectious disease area.

Three weeks later, Dr. Arnold called another meeting of the whole group. There was important news. In the course of his *Listening*, the internal medicine physician, a young newcomer to the hospital, had observed that the infection rates seemed highest among patients who had IVs in their hands and arms. The other members of the team were impressed, especially since there had been no outward sign that IVs were responsible for the patients' infections—no inflammation or swelling at the IV sites. The infections could have been from any source, but the young doctor had detected the connection to IVs.

He had also found that IVs were changed every 72 hours. At his previous hospital, the change had taken place every 96 hours, and he learned with a few phone calls that 96 hours was the state-wide norm. "The more often you change the lines," he reminded the group, "the greater the chance of infection."

Dr. Arnold shared the team's results with the CEO, who had asked to be kept in the loop. He suggested that supervisors in all areas of the hospital where IVs were in use should be asked to report back on whether their actual IV operations conformed to their written IV instructions. The CEO agreed and got the ball rolling. The supervisors' reports were back within a week, all of them insisting that the written procedures were being faithfully followed.

That left the mystery of the excessive IV infections unsolved, so Dr. Arnold asked his team members to go back to the *gemba*, this time focusing on areas of the hospital where IV lines were used. He also urged them to take the time to listen to what patients had to say about their IVs.

It wasn't long before the team made a series of surprising and disturbing discoveries:

- Different areas of the hospital were following different written procedures for the insertion of IV lines.

- Four different methods of site preparation were being used.

- Three different types of IV ports were being used.

- Many more than the expected number of employees were starting IVs.

- Patients with hand IVs were complaining of pain, and were asking that new lines be inserted as often as every two days.

The insights yielded in the Listen phase of LEO enabled Dr. Arnold and his team to develop a whole new set of proposals and strategies in the Enrich and Optimize phases. He presented them to the CEO with some nervousness because they called for a major revamping of the hospital's approach to IVs, but she quickly approved his plan.

A new written procedure to cover all hand and arm IVs was prepared and delivered to every department. A limited number of staff people, spread among the different departments, were trained in the new procedure for starting an IV line. After their training was completed, only they were permitted to insert IVs. And a single type of IV port was adopted for use with hand IVs.

Results

Because of these improvements, the hospital was able to adopt a policy of changing IVs every 96 hours instead of every 72 hours. That alone sharply lowered the rate of IV-caused infection. The policy also delivered some financial benefits. The 25 percent reduction in the number of IV changes cut hospital costs by more than $100,000 a year, and the lower infection rate shortened patients' average time in the hospital, saving the institution an additional $130,000 a year. The new process achieved through LEO was much more effective, reliable, and efficient.

The success in resolving the infection crisis was hailed in the local media. In an interview with a radio station, the CEO gave full credit to Dr. Arnold and his team. Back in her office, she called for a more rapid deployment of the LEO system throughout the hospital.

There was another, less tangible benefit from the IV project that only gradually became evident. As is true of LEO deployments in general, the experience of taking on a serious challenge and conquering it together inspired a greater sense of pride in the hospital's employees and a stronger we-can-do-it attitude. They have set themselves the goal of completely eliminating hospital-acquired infections.

> **As is true of LEO deployments in general, the experience of taking on a serious challenge and conquering it together inspired a greater sense of pride in the hospital's employees and a stronger we-can-do-it attitude.**

A PET FOOD COMPANY
LEARNS A NEW TRICK

The members of the product team responsible for the puppy brand at an East Coast pet food company were proud of their product. They were convinced that it provided all the nutrition that a puppy needed to set it on the road toward a healthy, happy maturity. They thought their customers, the puppies' owners, felt the same way.

The company's marketing people and salespeople had a different take on things. They were convinced that the time had come to produce a so-called premium puppy food. It would appeal, they argued, to affluent suburban customers who were willing and able to pay a bit extra for the comfort of giving their puppy the very best.

"Ridiculous," said the food scientist on the product team, a woman with more than 20 years of lab experience. She had analyzed the premium puppy food put out by a competitor and found that it was in no way healthier than her own company's product.

The other members of the team were divided on the matter. They included the product manager, a woman in her early forties with a pleasant demeanor, an impressive track record, and a no-nonsense style; two men in their early thirties with backgrounds in market research and sales; and a young man with a degree in packaging engineering. The young man had no strong feelings about the issue, which he considered "not my problem." One of the marketers thought the whole idea of premium puppy food to be a "silly fad."

The product manager leaned in that direction as well, but she knew that the proposal of the sales and marketing reps had a lot of research backing. They constantly presented her with their analyses of the research in the form of booklets and PowerPoint slides.

The pet food company tried to stay in touch with its customers in a variety of ways.

- **Surveys.** Puppy food customers were regularly sent questionnaires, by e-mail and regular mail, seeking their reactions to the current product and its rivals.

- **Focus groups.** Five to eight customers at a time were invited to respond to questions while seated in an office at the company's various sales centers. During the 90-minute sessions, the product team could watch and listen from another room; the customers were aware of that arrangement.

- **Personal interviews.** Market research teams would conduct individual interviews with customers that were billed as open-ended but that often ended up being Q&A sessions.

- **Field trials.** When the company developed a new or revised product, it was placed in selected stores to test customer response. There were also follow-up interviews with people who had bought the trial product to determine their reactions after using it.

The product manager had been through a LEO deployment earlier in her career. She remembered how powerful the Listen phase had been in guiding her toward the right path to take by intimately connecting her to her customers. That was when she decided that she and the other members of her team could not make a truly informed decision about the proposed premium product without directly listening to and observing puppy food customers in their natural habitat.

She split her team into three two-person units and arranged for each unit to visit the homes of several customers. There they had a chance to see customers go through the whole feeding process, from the opening of the puppy food package to the food's placement in a bowl to the reactions of the dog and the customer.

Result

For the product team observers, none of whom owned a dog, it was an eye-opening experience. "I feel I really understand our customers for the first time," one of them commented after the visits had been made.

One revelation was the depth of the customers' attachment to their pets and the seriousness of their commitment to their pets' health. That translated into a desire for puppy food that "looks" healthy and nourishing.

The team members gained two other insights, neither of which was particularly welcome. They watched aghast as several customers had trouble opening, handling, and closing the puppy food packages. And they discovered that most of the customers looked upon their puppy food brand as a low-cost product that was of no better than average quality.

The Listen experience opened their eyes to consequences. The product manager became a strong advocate for a new premium puppy food, and so did the other members of her team, including the food scientist. Once they understood the passion of the customers for their pets, the potential for a new product that appealed to that passion became obvious.

Once they understood the passion of the customers for their pets, the potential for a new product that appealed to that passion became obvious.

The time spent with customers also rid the packaging engineer of his blasé attitude. He realized that he had work to do. First, there was a clear mandate to redesign the existing product's package to make it more user-friendly. And the new product would also require some careful thought. One thing he was sure of—the packaging, while emphasizing the puppies' health, would also have to speak to the owners' love for them.

Review: Listen

1. Are you getting out from behind your desk? Go to where the action is. Go to the customers. Go to the factory. Go to the sales floor. Go to where the problems are. Go to where the facts are.

2. Are you doing all the talking? It's hard to listen that way. Watch what goes on. Watch what your employees are doing. Watch what your customers are doing. Listen to what they say. When you're confident that you've got it, watch and listen some more.

3. Are you empathizing with other people? Are you looking at the world through their eyes? Understand where your employees and your customers are coming from. It's not about you; it's about them. They're the people you should be listening to and learning from.

ENDGAME

There are any number of powerful management tools that can be used in the process of a Listen phase. But as is evident in the case studies in this chapter, the goal in a LEO deployment is always to keep matters as simple as possible.

The more complex the tool, the more effort a company must put into learning to use it properly, and the more difficult it is to tailor that tool to a company's particular circumstances. Put it this way: fewer complications means fewer things that can go wrong.

The fact is, the basic, no-frills techniques will do the job very well in most situations. As Leonardo da Vinci put it, "Simplicity is the ultimate sophistication."

The mandate to "keep it simple" applies to the Enrich and Optimize stages as well, but by their very nature, they invite the use of more complex management approaches. You'll see some of that in the next two chapters, the first of which is devoted to Enrich and the second to Optimize.

In the next chapter, the Enrich phase is shown at work at a bakery, a medical device manufacturer, and a maker of automotive seats. As usual, LEO is tailored to each company's special needs— and in one case, those needs were simple indeed.

Chapter Seven

ENRICHING THE PRODUCT

T he first coffeehouse in England was established in Oxford in 1650, and it turned out to be a good business—by 1675, there were more than 3,000 of them in England alone. At the same time, they were catching on all over Europe.

Coffeehouses drastically altered the public drinking habits of the day, turning their patrons away from their traditional reliance on beer, wine, and booze. The substitution of a stimulant for these depressive drinks awakened customers to serious discussion and debate, and that, in turn, inspired sweeping new ideas about everything from religion to politics. The coffeehouse was the breeding ground for what came to be known as the Enlightenment, which called upon humankind to put its faith in reason. Among its offspring was the American Revolution.

Then and now, in a coffeehouse or a corporate boardroom, the creation of valuable new ideas requires stimulation and a nurturing environment. And that process is central to the subject of this chapter—the Enrich phase of LEO. In the Listen phase, as you saw in the previous chapter, the emphasis is on pinpointing the customer's real needs and the real nature of the problem. In the Enrich phase, the search is on for the best solution. That generally takes some serious discussion and debate—and a lot of bright ideas. In the pages ahead, I describe how that happens in a LEO deployment—in general and in three case studies. It doesn't require a coffeehouse, but a cup of coffee wouldn't hurt.

In the Enrich phase, the search is on for the best solution.

I like to think of the Enrich phase as encompassing both meanings of the word. It makes products and processes better—it enriches them, introducing greater quality. And it thereby also tends to enrich the owners of the organizations that utilize this phase of the LEO process. Of course, such double applications of this word don't always work out. As we've all been taught, "Art enriches your life," but art is unlikely to do much for your bank account—far from it!

While I'm on the subject, I should point out that there is some more serious tension built into the two meanings of *enrich*, a tension that provides the ultimate test for any LEO deployment. Though the goal is to make the situation better, there are always practical limits. You're not going to enrich anyone if your improvement efforts disrupt things in your organization for weeks at a time—interfering directly with frontline processes, for example, or pulling too many people away from their regular assignments for too long. Nor are you going to boost the bottom line by devoting major resources to tweaking processes that have minimal impact on quality. That's why, at every stage of a LEO deployment, the team leader is expected to tally up the costs to date and make certain that they remain within budget.

> **You're not going to enrich anyone if your improvement efforts disrupt things in your organization for weeks at a time.**

One more essential element of the Enrich phase: it reflects LEO's commitment to continuous improvement, to the unending effort to achieve greater quality. Yes, the search for a solution to a problem must come to an end after a reasonable length of time, and some decision must be reached. But management should not be too easily or too quickly satisfied with the search results. LEO subscribes to the belief that there is always a better, yet-to-be-discovered alternative.

> **LEO subscribes to the belief that there is always a better, yet-to-be-discovered alternative.**

HOW TO GO ABOUT IT

The first stage of the Enrich process varies somewhat with the LEO mission. In Fire, it begins with a full statement of the specific problem. In Flow, the LEO team creates a map of the current operational situation. In Future, it starts with a study of the existing product or service design. In all cases, though, the goal is to identify and clearly understand what's happening—the "now" that was revealed in the Listen phase that is going to be enriched.

That can be more or less complicated, depending upon the mission. In Chapter 3, when putting out a Fire in a jelly bean plant, a *split-tree* analysis was used to rule out various possible reasons for the underweight jellies. In Chapter 4, a map of the existing request for quote process at the toy factory was put on the wall, with the various trouble spots called out. In Chapter 5, the brake supervisor put his team members through "an intensive program of study" to familiarize them with the brake system on the latest car model.

Once the current situation is in hand, the Enrich process calls for the development of alternative ways to solve the problem or go beyond the existing product or process. First, though, the team assigned to the project will typically tap all sorts of existing sources— from trade journals to the Internet, and from patent records to biology or chemistry books. Old ideas, long abandoned, may be given a fresh look. Data gathered from competitors will be carefully examined.

The Enrich process calls for the development of alternative ways to solve the problem or go beyond the existing product or process

From this research, a host of possible approaches to the particular problem will emerge. They will serve as the raw material for a series of sessions devoted to creating brand new alternative solutions.

Jamming

Some of these sessions will include *brainstorming*, a word that I'm not so fond of because it has come adrift from its original, serious meaning. In some circles, it's mocked as a wasteful, self-indulgent exercise. As used in a LEO deployment, however, it is a carefully prepared and conducted team meeting at which members are urged to give their imaginations free rein—about the matter at hand.

I actually prefer John Kao's word for the process: *jamming*. Kao, an authority on innovation, has been an entrepreneur, a Harvard professor, and a film producer. As a teenager, though, he was a talented jazz pianist who loved to jam with a group, the music spinning off in a dozen different directions, but always in relation to a single melodic theme. In effect, that's what happens in the Enrich phase of a LEO deployment. Team members riff on their melody—that is, the problem or product design that they're working on—in an environment that encourages and welcomes every conceivable new idea that is offered.

Team members riff on their melody—that is, the problem or product design that they're working on— in an environment that encourages and welcomes every conceivable new idea that is offered.

The basic notion is that among all the ideas presented, there will be some that are worth developing, and that among those that are developed, there will be at least one winner. The fact that so many ideas will be worthless is viewed not as a problem but rather as a necessary part of the process. For companies that live or die on innovation, on the constant creation of better, faster, cheaper products, inspiring a flow of new ideas is the core strategy.

A prime example is HTC, the Taiwan-based manufacturer of mobile phones. In its Magic Labs, 50 "magicians" from every part of the company—"chemical wizards" and "software wizards"—engage in brainstorming sessions. They are instructed to practice "zero learning," as the company calls it—to forget everything they know about a particular phone, for example, and approach it intuitively. In one case, the jammers were told to think about how people, including babies, interact with any object on the most basic level. The idea for the touch phone emerged from that session.

HTC is happy if, on a given day, the Magic Labs hatch hundreds of useless suggestions, as long as there's one valuable new idea. The notion that frequent failure is inevitable is built into the system. But to make the system work, this company—and any company—must create a set of unusual ground rules and stick to them. They are the same ground rules to be followed during the Enrich phase.

For its jamming sessions, the LEO team should work in a relaxed, informal mental environment. Team members should be encouraged to generate ideas without worrying about their practicality—without trying to figure out whether a given idea would be too costly in terms of time or money. In this free-floating discussion, every idea receives a full and respectful hearing; no idea and no person offering an idea is to be ridiculed. As HTC has discovered, some of the most seemingly outlandish notions have triggered some of its most profitable products. Indeed, valuable insights often occur in the process of debating ideas that will eventually be discarded.

Some of the most seemingly outlandish notions have triggered some of its most profitable products.

The physical environment needs to be conducive to idea generation—with comfortable seating, good lighting, and coffee and snacks at the ready. Team members should have materials available to give their ideas physical form, including pads and writing tools, monitor screens, whiteboards, and even prototyping materials such as clay.

To jump-start the creative process, teams may practice lateral thinking, reasoning that makes an end run around a direct, step-by-step approach to a project. Random word association, for example, calls for choosing a word or an object at random and associating it with the project you're working on. Or you might ask yourself why a random object exists in its present form and how it might be altered—this as a way to get your mind in an innovative groove before refocusing on the issue at hand.

TRIZ

Often, Enrich teams use a more structured tool like TRIZ, the creation of Russian inventor and science fiction writer Genrich

Altshuller. The letters come from the Russian; in English, the tool is generally referred to as Theory of Inventive Problem Solving. Early in his career, Altshuller was a patent clerk with the Soviet navy. As he pored over thousands of patents, he observed that in each case, one of 40 or so principles had been used to resolve inherent contradictions—for example, the fact that the wing of an aircraft must be both strong and light.

Using TRIZ, a team starts by clearly defining a problem and then looking for the contradictions and the appropriate principles needed to resolve them. The team then looks for examples of solved problems that shared contradictions with its own problem or applied the same principles. The approach used in those examples is then brought to bear on the team's problem.

Evaluation

Once these various approaches have inspired a substantial group of feasible design concepts—you should have at least eight or so— the Enrich team sets about evaluating them. Often, the Pugh matrix, which I described in Chapter 5, will be employed. Essentially, it measures how well each design satisfies the customer needs gathered in the Listen phase and how it compares to the company's current product design.

By the end of the Enrich phase, the team should have a new design that is significantly superior to its predecessor in terms of quality and performance while maintaining or decreasing its cost. The design will then move on into the Optimize phase, to undergo prototype testing and further polishing and cost cutting.

> **By the end of the Enrich phase, the team should
> have a new design that is significantly superior to
> its predecessor in terms of quality and performance
> while maintaining or decreasing its cost.**

Now, let's consider a problem confronted some years ago by a midwestern bakery.

A BAKERY BATTERED—BY ERRANT CUPCAKES

This regional bakery, which serves several states, has three plants dating back to the 1950s. Like the others, the cupcake facility is clean but not fancy, its dozens of employees bustling about in light green uniforms and hairnets. The bakery also boasts a modern food laboratory, an airy, sparkling new building where Ph.D. chemists and food nutritionists hold sway among the latest test equipment.

The bad news arrived at the cupcake factory in a report from the lab. Sample products from all three plants were regularly measured there for certain qualities. The mouthfeel, or texture, of the cream-filled cupcakes had been found to be badly inconsistent.

To determine the mouthfeel of a cupcake, the lab machines evaluate each major stage of its journey: palate, chewing, swallowing, and aftertaste. The texture of these particular samples had been all over the place—some fine, others too tough or too gooey.

The manager of the cupcake plant couldn't believe the lab report. As long as the plant followed the corporate recipe and obeyed the standard processing directions, there had never been a problem with texture—and he knew that the plant was on firm ground on both counts. The product manager believed the report. "I don't care how it happened or whose fault it is," he informed the plant manager. "I want the problem fixed, and I want it fixed now."

If he was going to find a solution, the plant manager knew, he would need to buy a machine that could constantly check product texture. But he found that there would be an eight-week delay in delivering the equipment, way too long to wait. Instead, he sent three of his people, one from each shift, to the lab to be trained in the use of an old texture-measuring machine that had been lying unused in a corner of his plant.

That took three weeks. By then, scores of customers had complained about biting into cupcakes that were overly tough or overly gooey. Once the newly trained inspectors began regular testing, they were able to catch and sideline most of the offending cupcakes, but at a cost: the amount of scrap (unsatisfactory cupcakes that must be discarded because they cannot be sold) soared from 0.8 percent to more than 5 percent, representing a loss of almost $10,000 a month. That pretty much wiped out the plant's profit.

The plant manager was under the gun. He was ordered to deliver daily reports on the status of the problem to the product manager, who had been ordered to share the reports in a daily phone call with the company president. In the blame game that ensued, the plant manager was "it."

He urged his top people to look for answers, and he himself spent long hours at the task. At one point, he contacted every supplier of raw materials for the batter (flour, baking soda, etc.) and for the filling (cream, butter, etc.) and demanded that they certify their materials. That required physical and chemical tests of random samples of their products, which could cost the companies thousands of dollars. About 20 percent complied, another 20 percent refused, and the rest adopted delaying tactics.

Elsewhere in the plant, chaos reigned. Line supervisors were trying their own solutions, adjusting the injection settings at the filling station or moving the baking time up or down. If the inspectors reported a batch of cupcakes that was too tough or too gooey, a supervisor might decide to change the batter mixing settings. It was a perfect storm of misguided trial and error that was simply making matters worse. The plant manager realized that he had to find a new approach.

It was a perfect storm of misguided trial and error that was simply making matters worse.

He created a small team of smart people he could trust who would work on the mouthfeel problem as close to full time as possible. He chose Len, the first-shift supervisor, to be the leader. Tall and fit, Len was in his early forties, although he looked a decade younger. He was a favorite with both the line workers and management and was the leading candidate to succeed the plant manager.

The other two members of the team were Alan, the second-shift supervisor, and Jennifer, the quality control supervisor. Alan, in his mid-twenties, had an associate degree in engineering technology from a local community college and was working on a B.S.

in engineering. A higher education was unusual in the plant, and Alan was a welcomed comer. Jennifer, in her mid-thirties, had never gone beyond high school, but she was admired by the line supervisors because she not only discovered quality problems but also usually found a way to solve them. As they put it, she was smarter than her job.

Cupcake manufacturing is not all that mysterious. The ingredients for the batter are mixed to the right consistency in a huge chamber and pumped through a pipe into a manifold with 18 nozzles. The batter is dispensed through the nozzles as three side-by-side cupcake pans on a conveyor belt pass beneath. Each pan holds 54 cupcakes.

The long line of three side-by-side pans then moves into an oven more than half the length of a football field, where they spend 20 minutes baking and another 20 minutes cooling. Then they go on to a station where 18 dies dip down to inject a creamy filling into each cupcake. The pans are then tipped over, and the individual cupcakes are transported via a conveyor belt to receive a frosting bath and additional toppings such as sprinkles. After some time in a cooling chamber to let the frosting and decorations firm up, the cupcakes are ready for packaging.

What's amazing, if not mysterious, about the process is the speed and precise timing with which the dispensing of batter and the injecting and frosting are accomplished—and the huge daily volume of cupcakes that they make possible.

At the first meeting of the three-person team appointed by the plant manager, Len asked the other members to join him on a walk along the line, from the last operation to the first, carefully observing what was happening and talking with the line workers. They even sweated their way through the hot room that houses the baking oven, checking to make sure that none of the banks of burners were down.

After their walk, the team members discussed what their first step should be. They agreed that all of the changes to the standard operating procedures and equipment settings should be canceled and the plant returned to the status quo. A well-defined starting point was needed. The plant manager agreed, and everything returned to normal—except for the texture of the cupcakes. The unwanted variations, from tough to gooey, remained.

Next, Len and his team listed the possible sources of the variations on a flip chart as a method of isolating the trouble spot along the line. They began with "shift to shift"—could the problem be limited to one or another of the three shifts that the plant worked? Next was "batter batch to batter batch"—was the problem a function of the composition of one or another batch of batter? That same way of pinpointing the location of the variations was to be explored in terms of the pans and the batter and fillings dispenser heads.

Len thought the list could be helpful, but he was very much aware that he lacked any real experience dealing with this particular kind of challenge, and he didn't want to waste the team's time on a wild goose chase. "I'd like to get in touch with Maureen," he told the others, referring to a shift supervisor at the company's bread plant. "I know she went through a management program that dealt with a problem something like this one. Maybe she'd come over and give us a hand."

As it turned out, Maureen had been through a LEO Fire deployment at her plant. Her first suggestion was that the team members develop another list. They were surprised at some of the pointed questions she asked along the way: "Is there one operator per shift on the batter mixer? Does the operator take breaks? Does another operator fill in during breaks?"

The first list jumped all over the map, from one site to another, with no logical order or sequence. Maureen's LEO-inspired list started by calling for a test of the measurement equipment used on individual cupcakes. It then gradually moved the hunt for variations away from the micro toward the macro: among cupcakes in the same row within a pan, then among rows in the side-by-side trio of pans on the conveyor belt, and so on until it sought for variations from one shift to another and, finally, from one day of the same week to another.

The team recognized the list as a step-by-step road map to follow, moving from one level of data collection to the next until the trouble spot was found.

> **The team recognized the list as a step-by-step road map to follow, moving from one level of data collection to the next until the trouble spot was found.**

The measuring equipment turned out to be accurate, and the team moved on to compare cupcakes, first in the same row and then among rows. They accomplished both items on the list by testing the texture of samples collected at random from rows in each of the three side-by-side pans. They discovered that among the 30 cupcakes sampled for each of the three pan locations, the left pans had 28 tough cupcakes, the right pans had 26 gooey cupcakes, and the center pans' cupcakes were fine.

"I knew it," Alan, the second-shift supervisor, exclaimed. "It's the differences in the heating zones of the oven. I've been after those maintenance guys to calibrate the burners every time they work on them, but they never do."

But Len wasn't so sure, and Jennifer came up with a way to test Alan's theory—by swapping the pans around before they entered the oven. So the center pans, which had had the good cupcakes in the previous test, were moved to the left, with the "gooey" right pans in the middle and the "tough" pans on the right. If Alan was correct, the pan switch would make no difference, but in fact it did. After passing through the oven this time, the cupcakes in the left pans were fine, while the middle and right pans had large numbers of gooey or tough cupcakes. The oven was not to blame.

Results

Eventually, the major suspects came down to the batter and filling mixers and dispensers. The team had a clue—the date when the troubles first began, by now three months earlier. They asked everyone they could think of, "What could have happened back in that period of time that might have thrown the system out of whack?"

Finally a member of the plant maintenance crew remembered receiving an e-mail around that time from an outside contractor who had been hired by the plant engineer to improve the piping system between the batter mixer and the batter nozzle dispensers. The work had been done over a holiday shutdown, so the maintenance people were not directly involved. As it turned out, the contractor's changes in the piping had increased the amount of time during which the batter was actually being worked, making it tougher. In fact, he had recommended that the time the batter remained in the mixer should be shortened to even things back up again.

What neither the contractor nor the maintenance people realized, however, was that the new twists and turns added within the manifold, which holds the dispensers, had further altered the equation. The result was wide variations in the texture of the batter delivered to the cupcake pans.

After duplicating the test to be sure that the team was on the right track, Len presented the results to the plant manager. Within a week, with the outside contractor's aid, the batter dispenser system was fixed and the mouthfeel problem that had haunted the cupcake plant for so long was resolved.

A SCALPEL MAKER MYSTIFIED—BY A SCANNER

A Mexican manufacturer of surgical equipment—scalpels, forceps, clamps, and such—maintained a 50,000-square-foot warehouse in El Paso, Texas. Truckloads of parts from U.S. suppliers were consolidated at the warehouse and shipped across the border to the company's five assembly plants in Mexico.

The warehouse could be a lively spot, with its 35 employees hopping, when the five truck unloading docks were filled with suppliers' vehicles and the five loading docks on the other side of the building were jammed with company trucks and impatient drivers.

To increase efficiency, the company introduced an electronic materials management system. Automating a good manual system can have drawbacks, but automating a bad manual system can be a nightmare. A wireless, handheld scanning gun picked up the bar code on an unloaded box and entered it into the system, where it was matched with an electronic version of the purchase order for the items in the box. When the match occurred, the supplier's account was automatically credited with a dollar amount equal to the agreed-upon price on the purchase order.

Automating a good manual system can have drawbacks, but automating a bad manual system can be a nightmare.

Simple, right?

A few months after the new scanning system was up and running, suppliers started complaining to the company's purchasing department. Some said that they were being underpaid for the parts that they'd shipped; others said that they hadn't been paid at all. The purchasing agent tried to find out what was going on, but the people at the warehouse blamed it all on the suppliers.

The situation rapidly deteriorated. Suppliers began refusing to ship parts until they were paid for the previous orders. That led to delays in delivery to the warehouse, which in turn led to spot shortages of parts at the plants in Mexico. Assembly lines were shut down. Machines and workers were idled. Money was lost.

In extreme cases, the vice president of the assembly operations would personally call the president of the particular supply company. Negotiations would be conducted in a spirit of ill will, usually ending with an electronic funds transfer to the supplier's account and the parts being shipped. The vice president ended up believing that the supplier company president was an extortionist, while the president of the supplier company thought the vice president was a would-be thief.

That was the situation when the scalpel manufacturer's top management arranged for a LEO deployment. A team of four was formed, including a warehouse supervisor and purchasing agents. They immediately scheduled Listen phase interviews with the people on the ground at the warehouse and at the suppliers. They discovered a series of snafus:

- If parts were ordered from suppliers on an expedited basis, the purchase order might not have been entered into the materials management system before the materials arrived at the warehouse. That prevented the scanned receipt from being properly entered into the system, so no payment was made to the supplier. The people working on the dock knew how to create a purchase order in the system, but they were often too busy to do so.

- When a purchasing agent placed a verbal or an e-mail order with a supplier asking that extra parts be added to a shipment, the agent often neglected to correct the purchase order in the system. The result was that the supplier was not paid for the extra parts.

- If the docks were very busy, the warehouse workers would sometimes let an incoming box get stored without scanning it. They would simply mark the box with a signal indicating that it had not been scanned and leave it to the staff at the manufacturing plant to scan the box into the system. When they were extra busy at the plant, though, such boxes sometimes never did get scanned into the system.

Two other factors complicated things. The company normally paid suppliers within 60 days after the shipment was received at the warehouse, but when shipments were not entered into the system upon delivery, that 60 days could stretch out to three or four months. That put the supplier in a cash squeeze—and a bad mood.

Also, the surgical equipment company was excruciatingly slow about responding to complaints of nonpayment. It often took a month for the company to find an error, another month to authorize the payment, and yet another few weeks to actually trigger the electronic transfer of funds.

Once the LEO team was grounded in the company's problems, the leader scheduled four meetings of two hours each. At the first, the members researched possible solutions in trade publications, in management literature, in industry best practices, and on the Internet. Another meeting was dedicated to brainstorming, using the materials from the previous sessions and the many fresh ideas hatched by team members. The next meeting was devoted to combining and synthesizing the best of the dozens of brainstorming ideas into the eight most promising system solutions. And in the final session, the team evaluated those eight systems on a Pugh matrix, settling on the three best before finally arriving at the best of the best.

Results

The team's proposal won the approval of the company's leaders. In short order, the company reduced its supplier payment terms from 60 days to 30, and two people were assigned to the El Paso warehouse to help out at peak times. As a result, virtually every supplier shipment to the warehouse was scanned and entered into the materials management system immediately.

The team also initiated LEO Flow projects to upgrade operations at the warehouse and to overhaul two key processes. Working with both the surgical equipment company and five of its key suppliers, the team drastically cut the time required to identify and react to supplier payment issues. And it redesigned the company's response to supplier inquiries about a nonpayment or an underpayment, improving both tone and efficiency.

With the electronic materials system now supported by effective processes at the warehouse and in the purchasing department, the relationship between the company and its suppliers was transformed, and the chaos in the company's operations quickly faded.

With the electronic materials system now supported by effective processes at the warehouse and in the purchasing department, the relationship between the company and its suppliers was transformed, and the chaos in the company's operations quickly faded.

A CAR SEAT COMPANY CONFUSED—BY TRADITION

A LEO deployment was under way at the automotive seat company, and the leader had asked the chief engineer a seemingly simple question. All of the elements for a new seat design were in place except for the adjuster, the device that changes the angle of the seat back. The LEO leader had inquired, "Could we have a few of your people to help us with an Enrich project on the adjuster?"

"Forget it," the chief engineer replied. "We don't have time to mess around. We'll just carry over our existing design."

On one level, the reaction was understandable. The traditional approach to looking at alternatives, at other ways of doing things, is in fact slow and frustrating. A group of designers or engineers sits in a room throwing out different concepts, arguing with one another over the merits of one idea or another, spinning off on a tangent. The process, which is akin to brainstorming, can be confused, unstructured, and endless.

> **The traditional approach to looking at alternatives, at other ways of doing things, is in fact slow and frustrating.**

That was what the chief engineer had in mind, and it didn't fit with his schedule. The entire design concept for the new seat had to be signed, sealed, and delivered to management within three weeks.

Results

The LEO leader—Jim, I'll call him—assured the chief engineer that he could work within that schedule, and after much discussion, he was given the services of two engineers for three hours a week over the following three weeks. In other words, he was given a total of nine hours of meeting time apiece to explore alternatives to the current adjuster and come up with a better design.

Using the tools of the Enrich phase, Jim and his small team looked at two different types of adjuster, a geared design and a cable-and-drum design. They were compared in terms of a dozen criteria, including crash safety. In plenty of time to meet the schedule, the team members developed a design concept that provided much improved performance at a 5 percent lower cost and also trimmed warranty costs by 50 percent.

It doesn't take a lot of time to find a better alternative if you have the right analytical tools and know how to use them. That's what happens in a LEO deployment. The chief engineer didn't understand that at first, but he does now. The improved adjuster design was a big hit with top management.

> ### Review: Enrich
>
> 1. Is everybody on the same page? Make sure that all team members are up to date on what was learned about customers' needs and wants during the Listen phase. Make sure everyone understands the current state of the problem or the design challenge.

2. Are you really thinking outside the box? The best solutions are not likely to be the ones you've tried in the past. To innovate, tap the imaginations of your people through no-blame, all-ideas-welcome brainstorming sessions. Then apply the LEO analytical tools to turn those ideas into reality.

3. Are you settling for less than the best? Set your sights high, and don't give up on the Enrich process until you have the solution or the design that will thrill your customers without breaking the bank.

ENDGAME

For company leaders, the Enrich phase requires a new mindset. After you have passed through the Listen stage, your horizons are open wide to possibilities that you had not seen before. But finding the right one for now, the idea that will achieve your immediate goal, requires that you alter your mental approach. As Albert Einstein put it, "Significant problems we face cannot be solved at the same level of thinking we were at when we created them."

For company leaders, the Enrich phase requires a new mindset.

To get the most out of the Enrich process, you need to embrace change and the idea that what you have now, and what you have done up to this point, simply isn't good enough. That's not so easy for anyone, and especially for executives whose every move is studied, analyzed, and critiqued by everyone else in the organization.

But there is a powerful message delivered to everyone when you sign on for change. It goes something like this: "Our company has to move beyond the status quo and adopt continuous improvement as our central strategy. And that goes for everyone in the company—including me!"

That's the attitude that a LEO deployment in general, and the Enrich phase in particular, calls for. It's the quality mindset.

In the next chapter, we move on to the final stage of LEO, the Optimize phase. There you'll see three organizations struggling to move their solutions and new designs closer to perfection with a little help from LEO—a photocopier company, a hospital, and a maker of jet turbine blades.

Chapter Eight

DON'T COMPROMISE; OPTIMIZE!

His son was off at school, and Philip Stanhope, better known as Lord Chesterfield, an eighteenth-century British statesman, sent him a series of letters whose wit and wisdom have stood the test of time. This is one of my favorites of his advice: "Aim at perfection in everything, though in most things it is unattainable. However, they who aim at it, and persevere, will come much nearer to it than those whose laziness and despondency make them give it up as unattainable."

As Lord Chesterfield suggests, there are two basic ways of thinking about perfection. Either it is the absolute best that anyone or anything is or could possibly be, or it is that which most closely approaches that state at any given moment. Generations of philosophers have argued that any perfect world would have to leave room for improvement.

LEO is dedicated to that second idea, to the goal of continuous improvement as a corporate strategy. And nothing so clearly demonstrates that dedication as LEO's third leg, the Optimize phase, which is the subject of this chapter. After all, it takes place, chronologically, after a team has come up with a method to put out the fire, or a solution to a flow problem, or a new product design. Essentially, Optimize says to a company or organization, "Congratulations! You've come a long way. Now, let's go all the way and make things even better."

> **LEO is dedicated . . . to the goal of continuous improvement as a corporate strategy.**

That is not always a popular position. The temptation to stop after the Enrich phase, to take the solution and run with it, can be hard to resist. It seems so natural to breathe a sigh of relief once you have a way to remove the immediate difficulty and simply apply the remedy—and forget the whole thing. Why delay for a second? Why spend more time and money trying to come up with a better answer? Why worry about the future when you feel you have barely enough time, energy, and resources to take care of the present?

The various answers to those questions all boil down to one word: *quality*. If you want to turn out high-quality products or services, the kind that will truly delight your existing customers and attract new ones, you need to keep raising the bar on quality. You need to keep straining toward perfection.

> **If you want to turn out high-quality products or services, the kind that will truly delight your existing customers and attract new ones, you need to keep raising the bar on quality.**

There is nothing really revolutionary about the idea of continuous improvement. It's what Lord Chesterfield preached back in the 1760s, and it's what Pat Riley, the basketball coach, has always urged his teams: "Excellence is the gradual result of always striving to do better."

Continually seeking performance excellence is hard work, and that's certainly true of the Optimize phase. In a LEO deployment, the obvious feelings of discovery and creativity come earlier, as you move toward and finally develop a robust solution or a new product design. But you must continue to examine the issues more deeply, with a perspective that is always challenging what you've created in the first place.

When you come to the very end of the Optimize phase and you look back, you realize that you've just accomplished something remarkable. The LEO tools have enabled you to substantially improve on your initial success—and to save the company a substantial amount of cash in the process.

That kind of result may not qualify as perfection, but it comes awfully close.

HOW TO GO ABOUT IT

I don't know about you, but when I go on vacation, I want things to go just right. Maybe it's because I have more time to be critical, but I get seriously annoyed over small issues that wouldn't bother me so much in the normal course of things. The hotel room at a resort can be comfortable and attractive, but if the shower doesn't work properly or the TV is on the blink, I get upset. Pity the manager who wants to know how I enjoyed my stay—I'm liable to give him an earful.

I remember talking with a resort executive who put it this way: guests can be happy with 90 percent of their visit, but that not-so-happy 10 percent can spoil their whole experience. "I know it's a cliché," he said, "but the devil is in the details."

That's true of so much in our lives, and it's certainly true in the business world. The new cell phone is perfect—except for the comparatively short battery life. The new food delivery service is ideal—except that it does a bad job with fish. The new supplier offers good value—but his communication system is messed up.

Things don't work—and *do* work—for the smallest of reasons, and that's why, in the LEO Optimize phase, the solutions and designs selected during the Enrich phase are torn down to their details. That's where their weaknesses can be found. Every component is combined and recombined to produce hundreds or even thousands of variations of the original solution or design. The resulting combinations are analyzed and prioritized.

In the LEO Optimize phase, the solutions and designs selected during the Enrich phase are torn down to their details. That's where their weaknesses can be found.

- Will they perform properly in spite of all of the potential enemies facing them out in the real world? You may recall the car brake example that I used in Chapter 5. In that case, the noise factors, the enemies, included overheating and customer misuse.

- Will they meet the needs and wants of their ultimate customers, as expressed in interviews and observations during the Listen phase? In the car example, the customers' needs included an easier-closing trunk and quieter brakes.

- Will they address the goals and limitations of the company itself? The new car brake design had to live up to safety standards, while also aligning with budget and warranty considerations.

So, the Optimize phase does demand some imagination on the part of the LEO team members. They have to be able to put their minds into a future framework in which the new solution or design is actually put into effect. That's not always obvious, especially with a product intended for a new target market.

At the heart of the Optimize phase, though, are analytical tools that are a powerful, routine element of the LEO system. I described one in particular in Chapter 5—the process pioneered by Genichi

Taguchi called robust optimization. This is the counterintuitive approach that tears apart solutions and designs down to their details and then builds them back up stronger without increasing the cost—and often decreasing it.

Even after robust optimization has done its work and an improved solution or design has emerged, it is further checked and rechecked with market testing or through other validation procedures. LEO holds that only after that kind of intense scrutiny and testing should a solution be put into effect or a new product placed in the hands of customers.

Yes, what I've described here—and what you will find in the case histories that follow—is a great deal more complicated and demanding than the traditional way of proceeding. How much simpler it would be to seize upon the results of the Enrich phase and put them right to work. Or so it might seem. But when the effects of the real world start to be felt, attitudes change.

The new brake design begins to overheat after 5,000 miles and shows unacceptable wear after 10,000. The engineers are called in to make a fix here, a fix there—but the fixes create new problems of their own. Instead of thrilling its buyers, the new sedan turns them off. Around the company, it acquires a nickname that isn't mentioned in the presence of management: the Lemon.

That has been the history of all too many of America's new processes and products. We need to change our ways and accept quality as our universal, everyday goal.

We need to change our ways and accept quality as our universal, everyday goal.

A COPIER COMPANY
GETS OUT OF A JAM

Back in the days when the LEO system was just evolving, a team of technical people at a photocopier company met to discuss ways of coping with a familiar problem: paper jamming.

"We could start the usual way by measuring the number of paper jams per 100 copies," one man suggested.

"You won't see any with this type of machine," another piped up. "You'll have to look at 10,000 copies at least—20,000 if it has a good paper feeder."

"That would take forever," someone else pointed out. "Just to check two or three design variations you'd be looking at 60,000 feeds."

The team leader shook his head. "Don't forget," he began, "some of the other operational problems affect the jamming. For example, I can cut the number of no-feeds by increasing the number of multifeeds."

A gloomy silence fell over the group.

Then one of the engineers, who was familiar with robust optimization, offered a suggestion. "We shouldn't be measuring the problem with the machine," he said. "We should be measuring the stability of the machine's function."

"I don't understand what that means," the leader said.

The engineer explained: any function is a transfer of energy, a signal and a response. The ideal design of a function would use all of that energy to carry out the function. So if you can find a way to measure the function of a product or a process, you should be able to vary its elements in order to move it closer to the ideal design—to optimize its function.

147

Any function is a transfer of energy, a signal and a response. The ideal design of a function would use all of that energy to carry out the function.

"Let's take the paper feeder," the engineer continued. "What, specifically, can we measure about the feeding of the paper?"

I should stop here and explain how the paper feeder worked. The photocopier used a roller, covered with a friction material, to move each sheet of paper along. To put it in robust optimization terms, in this particular transfer of energy, the drum provided the signal, and the movement of paper was the outcome.

In its search for ways to measure that movement, the team started talking about the motion of a piece of paper in the copier and the amount of energy involved. One team member Googled "laws of motion" to brush up on her knowledge of basic physics. Another offered an equation, $F = ma$, force equals mass multiplied by acceleration. And so it went for 30 minutes as the team leader carefully noted the various ideas and equations on a flipchart.

Gradually, after one flipchart was on the wall and another was half full, the ideas stopped coming.

"Look, people," the leader said, "we need to pull one measurable characteristic out of this mess that captures the purpose of the paper feeder."

The engineer came up with the answer: measure how far the paper moves forward when the roller turns.

The leader nodded his head in agreement, but then he had a question: "I understand that when the copier fails to move the paper

148

when it should, the measurement would be zero. What I don't understand is how to handle the case when the copier moves more than one sheet of paper at a time (a multifeed)."

That led to more discussion, but it was finally decided that if more than one sheet was moved, the total movement would be recorded. Given the normal movement of 20 mm, a multifeed of two sheets would be viewed as a movement of 40 mm.

In seeking to optimize the function of the paper-feeding mechanism, the team members had found a way to measure the outcome, the distance a sheet of paper moved through the paper feeder. Now they set about searching for a way to measure the signal, the rotation of the roller, that produced that outcome.

After considering nine candidates, they settled on the roller's so-called angular rotation—the distance through which it turns in the process of moving the piece of paper along. Like the angles in the circles we all encountered back in geometry class, the angle of the roller's rotation can be measured in degrees.

The team was now able to plot, on paper, the ideal function of the paper feeder, the perfect combination of signal and output measurements—a vertical outcome in millimeters and a horizontal signal in degrees. This proportion would be the standard against which any new paper feeder design would be judged.

"Great," the leader said. "So to find out the best design, we need to measure the movement of the paper under different roller angles, different signal levels—say 180 degrees, 360 degrees, and 540 degrees."

"Right," the engineer agreed, "but we also have to allow for the noise factors."

When customers used the copiers, they might use paper that was rough or glossy, light or heavy, and the roller surface might be new or worn. These uncontrollable elements would have to be considered. Since the machines were intended to be operated out in the real world, not just in the lab, they would have to be robust.

So, two categories of noise factors were created. One contained rough and lightweight paper and a new roller surface. This category is easy to move. That is, for a given amount of roller rotation, there should be more paper movement than in the other category. In that category, the paper was glossy and heavier, and the roller surface was worn. With heavy, slippery paper and a worn roller, there tends to be less paper movement for the same amount of roller rotation.

The team then ran a test of a proposed new paper feeder design under the three different roller angles, 180, 360, and 540 degrees. And under each of the angles, there were the two noise categories, one tending toward more movement and one tending toward less.

When the results were tabulated, the team's focus was on the difference in the distance traveled within each of the roller angle pairs. The most robust of the three pairings would be the one with the smallest distance between the two settings—the one that was least affected by the noise factors.

Results

This technique for separating the good designs from the bad ones, the wheat from the chaff, enabled the team to deliver a paper feeder that reduced both paper jams and multifeeds by more than 70 percent with no increase in cost.

In fact, the Taguchi approach soon spread beyond paper feeders to encompass all of the other 20 subsystems of copier design. It also changed the architecture of the company's campus.

One of the most imposing structures on the campus at the time was a football-field-size building where copiers and copier components were tested in runs of thousands and sometimes hundreds of thousands of sheets of paper. As a former executive described it to me, "Semi-trucks brought paper into one side of the building every day, and large waste haulers would take it away to the recyclers from the other side of the building." Today, he said, because of the company's widespread use of robust optimization, "The building is gone. It became green space. And our president bragged that because of robust optimization, our engineers could assess the quality of a copier using two sheets of paper."

Because of robust optimization, our engineers could assess the quality of a copier using two sheets of paper.

A HOSPITAL MENDS A BROKEN PROCESS

The management of a small community hospital was well aware that things weren't going as they should. The financial performance was so-so, the hospital's reputation within the medical community was low, and the general public was unimpressed. The administrator assigned her top people to look for specific areas of the operation where a significant improvement could be made.

At a meeting a month later in the third-floor boardroom, the executives made their reports. There were plenty of potential target areas to choose from, but the final selection was, on the face of it, a surprise: the hospital's hiring policies. Actually, it made a lot of sense.

Most of the people who had been hired during the previous year were nurses. Because of the hospital's high annual nursing turnover rate of 20 percent, replacements were constantly required. Departments struggled to stay afloat by assigning large amounts of overtime, but occasionally the nursing shortage was so severe that the emergency room operation had to be shut down. New patient admissions were lost as a result, and the bottom line suffered.

A LEO project was set in motion. A five-person team was formed, led by a 35-year-old executive whom I'll call Hank. To initiate the Listen phase, team members put together a detailed portrait of the existing hiring process. This is what it looked like.

The frontline supervisor completed a new employee requisition form in his computer and sent a hard copy by in-hospital mail to the human resources department. An HR employee checked the form, if necessary contacting the frontline supervisor for any missing information. That happened 40 percent of the time. Because of the supervisors' heavy workload, it took them an average of five working days to complete or correct the form.

The HR person then e-mailed the completed form to the appropriate manager, the director, and the hospital administrator. It took, on average, eight working days to get all those approvals. Hank and his LEO teammates were surprised to learn that about 60 percent of the approvals had been made by administrative assistants whose bosses had told them in no uncertain terms: "I don't have time for that."

The job opening was then posted for hospital employees, and after a suitable period of time, it was posted publicly. HR personnel screened applicants, forwarding information about promising candidates to the frontline supervisor and his manager for their review. Those who passed muster were interviewed by the HR manager, the frontline supervisor, and the supervisor's manager. The final candidates were given a job offer, contingent upon their passing a physical exam. Once they were formally hired, they attended a one-day orientation session and then went to work.

Hank and his team gathered any and all available data related to the hiring process, from the time the need for a new person arose because of a resignation, a transfer, or some other reason to the moment when the new person reported for work. The "lead time," as it was called, was an amazing 83 days, plus or minus 20 days. Direct hiring costs—locating, hiring, and orienting a candidate—were $3,100, which did not include overtime pay or the use of temporary or contract personnel.

The lead time was extended by 16 days because about 30 percent of the candidates ended up turning down the hospital's contingent job offer. And as much as three weeks could be added to the lead time waiting for an appointment for the physical exam; orientation was not begun until the exam results became available.

The closing of the emergency room because of the staff shortages, the LEO team determined, had lost the hospital about 95 admissions during the previous year—equal to revenues of more than $600,000. When that was added to the direct hiring cost of $740,000 and the overtime cost of $235,000, the potential opportunity for savings rose to more than $1.5 million.

And the dollar figures failed to encompass some very important intangibles: the negative effect of the hiring situation on the quality of patient care and the quality of the workplace.

Temporary people were seldom able to live up to the performance level of the regular team, and even the members of the regular team, exhausted from so much overtime, sometimes fell down on the job. The work environment itself, as one veteran nurse put it, was "no fun anymore." She was always working with new people—*strangers* was the word she used—and working longer than comfortable hours. She was also tired of having to break in newcomers.

Conditions were far worse than the LEO team members had suspected when they embarked on the Listen phase. As they prepared to enter the Enrich phase, Hank warned them, "It's not going to be easy, but we've got to find ways to make sense of this mess."

Over a period of weeks, the team developed a series of possible solutions:

- Ten-minute training videos for frontline supervisors on how to hire an employee would be put up on the hospital's internal computer system. They would include instructions for completing the computerized employee requisition form. Supervisors would have to pass a quiz on that subject before they would be allowed to submit a form.

- Drop-down menus would be added to the computerized form to give the frontline supervisor real-time help in filling out the form.

- Frontline supervisors would be given the names and contact information of people on all three shifts whom they could call for assistance with the employee form.

- Only the frontline supervisor and her manager would be required to approve the new-hire requisition before sending it to HR. The director and the administrator would learn about it at the weekly staff meetings.

- To cut back on candidate refusals, a single HR person would usher a job candidate through the whole hiring process, explaining the process at their first meeting, responding to any problems that the candidate encountered, and keeping the candidate up to date on how the process was proceeding from step to step.

- The wait for a physical exam would be reduced to four days by adding 20 or so of the 30-minute appointments to the physicians' schedules. Orientations would be conducted within that four-day period, since very few candidates failed the physical exam.

When the hospital administrator reviewed the LEO team's future-state map, she was impressed. So was one of her top aides. "I'm going to get moving on that video as soon as I get back to my office," he said. The administrator shook her head. "Not so fast," she replied. "The LEO project isn't over yet. There's still the Optimize phase to get through. Right, Hank?"

The team leader gratefully agreed. He understood the impatience to begin fixing the broken hiring process, the temptation to go with these initial results, but he knew that there was still work to do. "The whole idea is to keep topping yourself," he said. "You want to get your solutions as close to perfect as you can, and we aren't there yet."

155

The LEO team met several more times to improve upon their good start. Hank pushed them to rethink each of the changes in the future-state map. "What could go wrong with it?" he asked. "What would be a likely cause? What can we do about the cause?" Eventually, a revised version of the map emerged, including a whole new entry.

All through the project, the team members sought the input of other staffers. During a talk with Hank, one of the HR people suggested, "Why don't we just post internally and externally at the same time? We can give preference to internal candidates, but we can save a lot of time that way—and most jobs get filled externally anyway." That made a lot of sense to Hank, who wished he'd thought of it himself.

Other elements of the optimized map:

- After testing the instructional videos and the drop-down menus with small groups of frontline supervisors, the team made several adjustments in the proposals. In one case, after seeing how often the supervisors were interrupted as they tried to complete the requisition forms, autosave and autobookmark features were added to the software.

- To counteract the possibility that a supervisor couldn't reach an assigned contact person for help with requisitions, an independent cell phone number would be provided with a guaranteed callback time of 15 minutes. To make sure the contact people would be able to answer a supervisor's questions, they would be given training in the task. Also, a virtual meeting room would be established where the three contact people could exchange ideas for improving their performance.

- Because managers were sometimes unavailable to approve a requisition for a day or so, the team settled for a two-day approval cycle. But they also arranged for requisition requests to be placed in a red folder with the due date for approval written on it in large type—and for the folder to be displayed in a rack outside the manager's office. The move was explained as an effort to remind the manager to act on the request, but it was also out there where it could easily be seen by the manager's boss.

- Clear job descriptions were created for the HR people who were assigned to bird-dog candidates through the application process. For those portions of the HR job that were new, online training was developed and tested to make sure that the HR persons were excellent guides through the application process.

- Physicians were surveyed to make sure that they would accept the accelerated physical exam schedule. Several refused, but there were enough in favor to ensure that the four-day plan would work.

When he figured that the team had taken the optimization as far as possible, Hank arranged for the members to present their proposals and explain them to people in each area of the hospital. Instead of simply surprising people with a public announcement or at a formal meeting, the team wanted to prepare the ground, gathering support. They also took careful note of any objections they heard and, where feasible, made more revisions in the future-state map.

Results

Finally, Hank was satisfied, and the new-look hiring process was tested with 10 candidates. The results convinced the administrator that it should now be implemented. A year later, the results were tabulated, as follows:

- Lead time had shrunk from 83 days plus or minus 20 to 31 days plus or minus 5—an improvement of 62 percent.

- Turnover rate had dropped from 20 percent to 12 percent.

- Direct hiring costs had fallen by $485,000, while the savings on overtime and part-time staff had reached $107,000.

- Bed utilization had risen 50 percent, for a gain of more than $300,000.

- Patient surveys showed a rise in quality-of-care ratings from 3.4 to 4.3 on a 1-to-5 scale.

- Employee surveys showed a rise in morale ratings from 2.6 to 3.9 on a 1-to-5 scale.

The administrator was "thrilled," as she put it, by the outcome of the project, especially because of its effect on patients' and employees' attitudes. Nor did the total savings of almost $900,000 escape her notice.

She was also impressed by the changes in the proposed solution between the Enrich and Optimize stages. "When I first heard about Optimization," she said, "I thought it was just sort of an add-on, a polishing up of the decisions reached in the Enrich stage. It was a great deal more than that. We wouldn't have made anywhere near as much progress without it."

"When I first heard about optimization," she said, "I thought it was just sort of an add-on, a polishing up of the decisions reached in the Enrich stage. It was a great deal more than that. We wouldn't have made anywhere near as much progress without it."

A week after the one-year results were in, the administrator called Hank and his team into her office. She praised them both for their success and for the careful way they had gone about it. The team was leaving, their faces aching from so much smiling, when the administrator held up her hand.

"Just one more thing," she said. "We're planning on doing another LEO project pretty soon, and you're obviously the right people to make it work."

A BLADE MAKER UPGRADES ITS COMPETITIVE EDGE

Most of today's airliners rely on turbofan engines, and the back ends of turbofan engines rely on rows of turbine blades. No surprise, those blades have to be really tough, capable of long-term, reliable performance under impossibly hot (2,000°F) and high-stress conditions. At the same time, they must meet extremely tight design tolerances—they have a very complex geometry, including cooling channels and thin trailing edges.

To improve on its already well-demonstrated ability to turn out these blades, a midwestern company turned to LEO and robust optimization. Like the five-inch-long blades themselves, this optimization had a special twist.

Before we get to that, though, I need to explain some basic facts about these turbine blades. To begin with, to produce these complex, high-tech objects, the company relies on a process that was first used around 400 BC: lost-wax casting. A wax model of the turbine blade is made and covered by a slurry of ceramic materials that harden into a mold. The wax is then melted out of the mold, and molten metal is poured in. When the mold is broken open, what remains is a perfect duplicate in metal of the wax model.

About that metal: it's a superalloy. Like any metal, it has a grain structure, much like wood, each grain consisting of a single crystal of the alloy. Naturally, the strongest blades will have a single crystal. That's because the boundary between two crystals is inevitably a weak link, one that is more likely to fail under pressure.

The company's engineers had been producing blades whose single-crystal percentage was 92 to 95 percent, and they wanted to do better. A LEO team was organized, and the members conducted any number of designed experiments, varying different aspects of the lost-wax process and measuring the results on the single-crystal percentage. The results were disappointing. Even when the lab experiments showed a 98 percent result, when the changes were applied in actual production of the blades, the percentage reverted to the 92 to 95 level.

The LEO team leader, a middle-aged engineer who had been working with the blades for a decade, finally took the problem to an authority on the robust optimization process, who engaged him in a Socratic dialogue:

"Why are you measuring single-crystal percentage?"

"Because that's what we want to improve," the team leader replied.

"What's the purpose or function of the lost-wax process?"

"To create a metal part in the shape of the wax mold."

"Then measure wax dimension versus metal dimension."

"I tried that, but the turbine blade's geometry is too complex to get accurate measurements of its dimension."

"Then make a part that's easy to measure."

That was the project's special twist, and when the leader told the members of his team about it, they were not impressed. What was the point, they asked, of trying to solve a problem by going around the barn door versus going through it? In other words, what was the point of measuring something other than the turbine blades themselves? So the team conducted an even larger designed experiment, altering the number values for even more of the molding process. It took a whole year, and it produced the same, unsatisfactory 92 to 95 percent result.

What was the point, they asked, of trying to solve a problem by going around the barn door versus going through it?

Finally, the team leader insisted upon the special twist suggested by the robust optimization authority. Within two days of meetings, the team had designed a new robust optimization using a wax model with easier-to-measure dimensions. Twenty-three numerical values for the lost-wax process—the composition of the wax and the ceramic slurry, for example—were altered and applied to 36 wax molds. The effect of the changes on the resulting 36 metal pieces was measured before and after they were exposed to a temperature of 700°F in a stressed condition. The most robust settings were identified, and the whole operation took a month.

Results

The optimized measurement of the lost-wax function revealed 12 process settings that needed to be changed when casting the actual turbine blades; 11 other settings were retained. When the new settings were tested, the resulting blades were twice as stable and much closer to the dimensions of the wax model. And most important, the single-crystal percentage rose to 97.

"That's just in the test parts," one of the engineers commented. "We'll see what happens in production."

As it turned out, the single-crystal percentage that had for so long remained at 92 to 95 percent rose to 95 to 97 percent during production. Improving the function of the process that created the blade was the best, the fastest, and the least costly way to improve the quality of the blade.

> **Improving the function of the process that created the blade was the best, the fastest, and the least costly way to improve the quality of the blade.**

Review: Optimize

1. Are you ready to accept perfection as your goal? If you want to raise the quality level of your products or processes, and keep raising it, you need to set the bar high, both for yourself and for everyone in your organization. Average is not the goal.

2. Are you willing to worry? Yes, optimization can greatly improve the decent solution that emerged from the Enrich phase, but the results must be filtered through a kind of protective paranoia. Keep asking: "What can go wrong? Will it work out in the real world?"

3. Have you prepared your team for the excitement of optimization? Make them understand why that decent solution has to be treated as a starting point, and why the extra effort toward greater quality at reduced cost will benefit everyone, customers and employees alike.

The extra effort toward greater quality at reduced cost will benefit everyone, customers and employees alike.

ENDGAME

The Optimize phase is literally the endgame of the LEO deployment. It is the time for making as sure as you possibly can that you've taken your solution or your improved product or process as far as you possibly can. What happens at this stage of LEO will determine the extent of the benefits you receive, so you need to throw yourself fully into it. In other words, it's the time for giving the process your all. As Euripides, the Greek playwright, put it, "He who strives will find his goals strive for him equally."

The Optimize phase is literally the endgame of the LEO deployment.

I understand that robust optimization can seem puzzling and counterintuitive. American companies have been slow to adopt the approach, even though it has been widely practiced in Japan for years. But once the basic thinking behind it is understood, robust optimization makes perfect sense.

I'm thinking of a blade that is very different from those used in turbine engines—a windshield wiper blade. I'm sure it has happened to you as it has to me: you're driving in a misty rain, you turn the wipers on, and instead of smoothly cleaning away the water, they sort of chatter, or vibrate, as they move across the glass.

Your first inclination is to measure and adjust the speed of the blade, which typically will correct the chatter but will also reduce the blade's ability to remove water from the windshield. It's so much more efficient to measure the function or purpose of the blade, which leads you to measure the ability of the motor to position the blade correctly. That's where the best total solution will be found, one that fixes the immediate problem without creating any new ones.

In the next chapter, you will discover a deployment with a very different goal: the transformation of a company's culture.

For such a full-scale engagement with LEO to succeed, the CEO and the rest of top management had to make a firm commitment to the project. That meant understanding and then practicing LEO concepts in their own behavior and taking an active and continuing role in promoting these concepts throughout the organization. It was not a walk in the park, but as the CEO of this consumer products company learned, the outcome was definitely worth the effort.

Chapter Nine

AN ALL-OUT LEO DEPLOYMENT

O ne rainy night in Manhattan, I was having a late dinner with the CEO of a sizable consumer products company. He had been in the job for five years or so following a long career with General Electric. We were sipping coffee after the meal when he began talking about a management dilemma that he couldn't seem to resolve.

The CEO wanted to change his company's whole culture to make it more customer-centric, and he knew that Six Sigma could help in that regard. But there were a couple of problems. "To start with," he said, "I'm not Jack Welch. Aside from that, my people's knowledge level just isn't high enough for them to handle Six Sigma. It's too complicated."

Eventually, he turned to me with a question: "Do you know of any way to work a real, lasting culture change that's not so hard to get your arms around, that's not so technical?"

I did.

Several months later, the CEO and I signed a contract for a full-dress LEO deployment at his company. We promised that the deployment would transform the corporate culture, given the full support of the project by him and his top aides. We also promised that, based upon our studies of the performance of the manufacturing plants, the organization would realize a savings of at least $85 million within 18 months.

This chapter tells the story of that total deployment. As it happens, the company involved operated 12 plants with 20,000 employees, but as I pointed out earlier, one of the most important things to know about the LEO approach is this: it can be tailored to the needs and circumstances of virtually any company of any size, whether it be product- or service-oriented, profit or nonprofit. It can work as a full monty deployment for the entire organization, or on an in-and-out basis to cope with a single problem—or anywhere in between. And it is designed to aid company leaders in meeting their goals while raising shareholder value by reducing costs, lifting revenues, and increasing profitability.

The LEO approach . . . can be tailored to the needs and circumstances of virtually any company of any size.

In that first conversation with the CEO, I asked him whether he was willing to learn the LEO system and personally lead the deployment. "Wait a minute," he replied. "How am I ever going to find time to study all that, even if I could understand it? And anyway, that's a job for my vice president of development." I assured him that LEO was not Sanskrit, that he could easily master the essentials.

I also listed the four key aspects of a full-scale LEO deployment that he and his top executives would be responsible for:

1. **Commitment.** Become active, knowledgeable participants in the planning stage, strong advocates for the LEO approach, and partners in the LEO deployment itself.

2. **Consistency.** Closely monitor the progress of the deployment to make sure that its goals and procedures are honored—and that personnel and financial resources are available as needed.

3. **Competency.** See to it that the training programs, including the individual LEO projects, are producing leaders who can maintain the LEO system post-deployment. Establish an environment of trust and patience during the deployment.

4. **Communication.** Use every means available, from the intranet to town hall meetings to personal workplace visits, to express your commitment to LEO and to spread word of the deployment's progress. Foster two-way communication to elicit feedback, good and bad, concerning the deployment.

The CEO, understandably, thought that this was a lot to take on. But the more he came to understand LEO and the deployment, the more doable it seemed. The demands on his time wouldn't be more than 5 percent, the disruption to the plants' operations would be minimal, and the big dollar savings would come in handy, given the recession. So he took the plunge.

As Ray Kroc, leader of McDonald's during its march across the globe, so wisely, if ungrammatically, observed, "The quality of a leader is reflected in the standards they set for themselves."

SETTING THE STAGE

The first step here, as in any full-dress LEO deployment, was to create an infrastructure in each of the dozen plants—a process that required three weeks. To set the stage, a team of five people was assembled at corporate headquarters, three of them from the company and two of ours.

Those from the company were all longtime employees in their late forties who were ready to work hard and were savvy about the organization. Their regular jobs were in finance, continuous improvement, and operations. As senior managers, they had enough clout so that they didn't have to call 10 people before making a decision. Working with a large organization, you always have to worry whether your company partners will behave as though a penny-pinching executive is constantly looking over their shoulders. That wasn't much of a problem here.

Our two people were LEO veterans, each of whom had completed more than 10 such deployments. One of them, who was 37, had a degree in industrial engineering. The other, in his mid-fifties, had degrees in electrical and computer engineering.

This team began by drawing up a mission statement, Standard Operating Procedure (SOP) for LEO deployments. Among other things, it promised to "drive a sustainable culture of continuous improvement" and equip employees "with the skills and tools needed to achieve year-on-year cost savings while generating a pipeline of future improvement opportunities." The $85 million savings figure was prominently displayed.

More important than the specific language of the mission statement, though, were the signatures of the company's top executives that appeared on the document. When the CEO ordered the deployment, he made it clear to the members of his management team that he wanted the project to have their active support. That message was passed down through the ranks to everyone in the organization. But by signing the mission statement, he and his executive crew were putting themselves on record, as it were—and that record became an integral part of the deployment. It was shown in the house organ, on the intranet, and at the start of every training course.

Why? Because no deployment is going to succeed unless the executive cadre is actively supporting it each and every day. And that holds for every corner of the company. LEO is not just for the engineers—it has to have the support of the accounting and marketing and legal and financial vice presidents as well. If an organization is to truly benefit from a full LEO deployment, the commitment to quality and continuous improvement must first be made at the top. That's where everyone else in the organization looks for leadership. If people believe that the deployment is just another SOP to appease the board or an effort by the CEO to cover for a weak fourth quarter, they will not fully engage, and the LEO initiative will fail.

No deployment is going to succeed unless the executive cadre is actively supporting it each and every day.

The next task for the team of five was to put in place a command structure for the deployment, both the individuals who would play leadership roles and the members of the project teams. For the deployment as a whole, the CEO was the company's CEO, while the plant managers at the various locations functioned as CEOs of their deployments.

The company's chief was a no-nonsense executive who wasn't interested in wasting any time or beating around the bush. His favorite phrase was: "Tell me like it is." He was the lead communicator and advocate for the deployment—attending training sessions, providing resources as needed, and eliminating roadblocks. He also monitored the progress of the program, not only from his desk but also in occasional visits to the areas where LEO was being taught and practiced.

Every deployment needs a majordomo, someone high up in headquarters who will back up the CEO, devoting 10 percent or so of his time to monitoring and promoting the program and resolving problems on a daily basis. Call him the deployment leader.

In this case, the leader was an operations vice president, a take-charge type with a business school degree. He fielded problems that couldn't be resolved at the plant level, kept an eye on day-to-day progress, and conducted overview sessions at which employees who were not directly involved in the deployment learned what it was all about. Attendees walked away with a positive view of the program. When project teams were looking over a piece of machinery, nearby workers would come over. "Are you those LEO guys?" they'd ask. "Want to know about why that machine failed an hour ago?"

Next, the team of five had to see to the selection of the project leaders, an average of 40 per plant. Each of them would, as part of his LEO training, take on a project to improve the efficiency of an individual process. The project leaders had to be line managers, responsible for significant production resources, with enough stripes to make decisions quickly and on their own. At the same time, the deployment team was looking for people who had a passion for the work and were open-minded, natural leaders.

That's why Paul, as I'll call him, was chosen. He was tall, and at age 47 he could still bench-press 200 pounds pretty much forever. He had a degree in education, yet he'd ended up managing a production line at the company's flagship plant. He didn't wear any stripes on his sleeve, but he was a leader, somebody who people listened to—though he wasn't listening to us at first.

In addition to the project leaders, some 70 people in each plant had to be picked to serve as members of the project teams. They were line people who had demonstrated their intelligence and skill level.

Finally, an overall work plan had to be put in place. It included

- A list of existing or scheduled company initiatives to make sure that there was no duplication or conflict with LEO activities.

- A schedule for the separate training sessions for executives, team leaders, team members, and the company as a whole.

- A process for tracking the hundreds of LEO projects. That included project proposals, approvals, progress reports, completions, and benefits in terms of dollars, process improvements, and culture change.

- A blueprint for communicating LEO news and encouragement to participants in the deployment.

The team of five started its infrastructure labors working from a generic LEO deployment plan, but of course this plan was amended and reshaped again and again, as usual, to deal with the particular company personnel and circumstances.

In creating the work plan, the deployment team never forgot a vital aspect of a LEO deployment: it's front-loaded. The media always make much of the first 100 days of a presidency, because that's when America's newly elected chief executive has the greatest momentum. A deployment, too, has to gain traction within those first few months if it is to make its mark.

A deployment . . . has to gain traction within those first few months if it is to make its mark.

Any time you introduce a new program to an organization, there is going to be some resistance. Unless that negativity is nipped in the bud quickly, resistance can spread like a weed and threaten the whole program. Also, the support and participation of the CEO and his top executives are greatest at the start and tend to taper off.

By the end of the third week, the deployment infrastructure was in place. It was time to start finding projects for each of the company's 12 plants. This would take two months.

PRIMING THE PUMP

To come up with all those ideas for LEO projects, the members of the team of five went into overdrive, using the Listen segment of LEO. They and their counterparts at the individual plants pored over performance data, studying scrap figures, downtime, overtime, reports of damage, and other negative variations from the norm. They left their own offices to visit line employees in other offices and on the factory floor, talking with the people who actually operate the processes.

They were not looking to tear up the pea patch. The goal was to develop projects that rooted out waste, but the scope of each project was carefully weighed. If it wasn't a significant improvement, there would be no sense pursuing it, and the person running the project would be uninterested in it, if not bored, and apt to botch it. If the scope was too broad, the effort too challenging, it was also likely to be a failure. In other words, the goal was not to reinvent the place but rather to integrate the waste-saving, customer-oriented methods of LEO into the organization.

The goal was not to reinvent the place but rather to integrate the waste-saving, customer-oriented methods of LEO into the organization.

As opportunities for projects were spotted, the details were set down on a standard form. It included a description of the project and its scope, the objectives in terms of the particular process, and a dollar figure representing the likely cost saving. Though the financial side was important, the focus was more on achieving greater efficiency with each project. Too much concern with dollars inevitably leads to shortcuts and shoddy performance.

High-quality projects lift performance, the best and most certain path to satisfied customers and financial success.

About now, you may be wondering why it was necessary to develop so many project ideas before the training of company personnel in the LEO system even began. Wouldn't it have made more sense to train them and then work with them to find appropriate projects in their individual work areas?

Good question. The answer: once they had a few days to become familiar with their future project, it provided them with a concrete reason to attend class. Instead of its being an abstract experience—just another guy in authority yakking at them, telling them what to do—they saw the class as helping them prepare to get the project done.

Those early projects were also a way of priming the pump. Once the project leaders began working with LEO on their projects, they inevitably saw other projects that were worth doing. The project pipeline began to fill up with new money-saving proposals. As in every full-dress deployment, that is the larger purpose. The CEO of this company wanted his $85 million savings, for sure, but he also wanted to see the LEO approach adopted throughout the organization.

In spite of the time deadline and the large number of projects required, each of the proposed projects was put through a careful validation process, including an examination by the financial wizards to make certain that the anticipated dollar savings were reasonable.

EXECUTIVE SESSIONS

By the time the team of five was ready to start the actual training process at the flagship plant, the company's employees were well aware that something major was brewing. The whole process of selecting project leaders and teams and exploring the dozen plants for pump-priming projects had everyone buzzing.

The first employee who learned about LEO, of course, had been the CEO. He had naturally wanted to know what we could do for him. That meant that we had to become familiar with the company's operations, including its problem areas. When he heard our recommendations, he wanted to know precisely *how* LEO worked. Finally, he was ready to commit himself and his organization to a full deployment.

That personal commitment is essential to the success of any total LEO deployment. If the leader is behind something, and constantly and strongly demonstrates that support, her troops are going to follow suit. It's just human nature. We all start out in life trying to please our parents, and most of us end up in organizations where we try to please our bosses. We look to our leaders for clues to how we should behave. If the CEO says to get behind the LEO deployment, the program is going to be on track.

Personal commitment is essential to the success of any total LEO deployment.

But if the program is to stay on track, the CEO has to follow through on his commitment. He has to stay on top of the program, attending progress sessions, questioning and challenging his aides, and personally making his presence felt in the company's various plants. For him to fulfill that role, though, he must have a crystal-clear understanding of the LEO approach.

Too often, CEOs convince themselves that they can wing it, and they pretend to know everything about major aspects of their organization. They preside over meetings that are devoted to marketing or engineering issues, confidently listening and asking questions, calling for greater efficiencies—while their executives exchange amused or embarrassed glances because their boss is asking the wrong questions or making ill-informed comments. When that happens, the organization suffers. The executives lose confidence in the CEO's leadership. They leave such meetings without clear guidance concerning how to deal with the issues that were raised. And they don't worry so much about delivering the goods when they go to the next meeting with the CEO.

For much the same reasons, if a CEO is unwilling to invest the time and energy it takes to understand LEO, she cannot effectively lead a full-scale LEO deployment. If she doesn't care enough about LEO to become smart about it, why should her top aides bother to do so? And that is the death knell for any in-depth deployment. That's why we will not proceed with one unless a company's leader truly does comprehend the LEO system.

> **If a CEO is unwilling to invest the time and energy it takes to understand LEO, she cannot effectively lead a full-scale LEO deployment.**

Deployments also rely on the commitment of the CEO's aides, the company's top executives. There were about 50 of these leaders, including the managers of the 12 plants, on hand at a one-day interactive workshop session at the consumer product company's headquarters.

The leader of the session started things off with a question: "If I have a process that makes 100 pieces a day, and 90 of those pieces are good and 10 are bad, should I throw away the equipment?" Almost all the executives said no. The leader repeated his question a few times, gradually lowering the number of good pieces; gradually more and more of his listeners voted to throw away the equipment. Finally, with the process turning out just a single good piece, everyone in the room was ready to give up on the equipment.

"That's the wrong answer," the leader told them. "I set you up. The LEO answer is, if a process is capable of making a single good piece, your job is to find out why it isn't doing so consistently. That's what you can do with the LEO tools."

Though there was a lot of give and take during the workshop, the leader was careful not to ruffle any feathers. He wanted to engage with the executives, to make sure that they understood the LEO fundamentals, but he also didn't want to embarrass anyone. He needed to have these people on his side during the deployment.

Communication Is the Key

The tough questions were saved for later, at individual meetings with the top people every two weeks or so. During those sessions, with nobody else in the room, the LEO training could be more direct. One aspect of LEO that executives sometimes have trouble with is Listen: Observe and Understand.

I remember sitting in a staff meeting with a senior vice president during another deployment. He brought up a topic, and I could tell from their body language that a number of people in the room disagreed with his position, but they didn't say a word. Later, I talked with him about my observation. He was surprised, and after that he would go around the room at meetings, asking for reactions to his ideas. I listened, and he learned.

The sessions with the CEO and his senior aides emphasized the ways in which they could get across their support of the deployment as well as information about its progress. That communication is essential to the success of the deployment. It can be accomplished through all the usual channels, including newsletters and posters, but the executives were urged to integrate the LEO deployment into their everyday work lives—discussing the latest developments or praising a particular LEO initiative at every staff meeting, and scheduling regular visits to LEO classes or a project review session.

> **Communication is essential to the success of the deployment. It can be accomplished through all the usual channels, including newsletters and posters, but the executives were urged to integrate the LEO deployment into their everyday work lives.**

Some executives actually pursue a project of their own. It's by far the best way to understand how LEO works.

At one of the company's plants, for example, the chief financial person undertook a project to unravel a mystery: there was a substantial discrepancy between the number of items listed in inventory and the number that showed up in physical audits. As it happened, he was the kind of person who preferred working on papers with his office door shut, who had trouble looking people in the eye. He became more outgoing, of necessity, in the course of the project, especially because he had to talk to a number of people in the Listen phase. Once he had completed the project, he became one of LEO's biggest boosters.

BASIC TRAINING

The training time for project leaders will vary from one deployment to the next, depending upon the company's particular circumstances. At the flagship plant, it was five days, which was about four days too many for Paul, the leading Doubting Thomas among the operations managers and line supervisors who took part in the classes. He believed that LEO was just another meaningless management exercise—"the flavor of the month" is how he put it.

Project Leaders

About 40 people from each plant eventually went through the project leader training, with classes generally including 8 or 10 students from one or more plants. The total registration for all plants represented 35 percent of the company's exempt employees.

To give Paul his due, he showed up for each day of class on time and stayed the course, as it were, although early on he behaved as though he were doing us a favor. One or two others among the trainees at the flagship plant were not so accommodating; they simply failed to appear on the second day, assuming that they could ride out any storm that ensued. They would simply insist that they had "more important things" to take care of. The class leader would contact the plant manager; after he read them the riot act, they returned to class the next day with a different attitude.

The atmosphere in the project leader workshops was far more animated and informal than at the executive sessions, and also far more detailed in terms of LEO principles and tools. There was no problem about ruffling feathers here. The students had each been assigned a project, and they were motivated to find out how they were expected to go about completing the project LEO style. If that meant being challenged to absorb new concepts and new ways of looking at problems, so be it. At the end of each class, the leader was deluged with questions about the students' individual projects. He assured them that a LEO veteran would be there to coach them through the start of their first project—not from the sidelines, but with them out on the field.

For many people, connecting fully with LEO is something like learning to ride a bike. You keep trying and keep trying—and then, suddenly, something clicks, and you're a rider forever after.

"When you have a problem, you usually think for a while and make an educated guess as to how to fix it," the deployment leader said. "If that doesn't work, then you try something else. And if it's a simple problem, that might work. But most problems aren't so simple. With LEO, there's no guessing. It's all logical, deductive reasoning."

With LEO, there's no guessing. It's all logical, deductive reasoning.

Put it this way: if you're trying to find out the number of jaw-breakers in a bottle, you can try to count those that you can see and then come up with an estimate that is almost sure to be wrong. But if you can find out the volume of the jar and the volume of a single jawbreaker, you're going to come a lot closer.

Occasionally, someone will come along who grasps LEO almost intuitively and spurns any coaching. I remember a plant manager who, after sitting through a training session and reading some LEO materials, went off on his own toot, spotted a promising project, and applied the LEO tools to complete it. We weren't sure whether to be pleased—or annoyed because we were suddenly redundant.

For most of those who attend the project leader workshops, though, it takes some time to learn the LEO approach. At the company's flagship plant, Paul was faster than most in that regard; by the third day of his workshop, he had left his doubts so far behind him that he was proposing new ideas for future projects. It wasn't long before the other students were doing the same thing.

Every so often, at one or another of the company's plants, the workshops would have an unannounced visitor—the CEO. When he showed up, everything stopped cold, but he would always insist that the class proceed. At the end of the class, though, he would turn to one of the students and ask him some questions. "Have you personally talked with all your line workers about LEO?" was a favorite. When the student admitted that she had not, explaining that she had been so busy with her LEO project, the CEO would keep boring in: "That's no excuse. This whole LEO program depends upon you project leaders. We're counting on you."

Project Team Members

Workshop sessions for the project team members were less intensive than the project leader variety. They lasted just two days, and they were entirely theoretical, since team members had no projects of their own. The mission was to give them enough background on LEO so that they could help the leaders—who were usually people that they already reported to—with their projects.

Still, many of the 700 or so students became enthusiastic backers of the deployment. Several asked if they could be allowed to take the training to become project leaders, and many of them suggested possible LEO projects at their plants. One woman, a graduate of a team member workshop at the flagship plant, told the CEO, "I've had this idea for fixing a process for years now, but I never felt that anybody would listen. After seeing how LEO is changing things, I finally feel comfortable talking about it." Her idea for improving a packaging process ended up saving the company $400,000.

During the first three months, the vice president, who was backing up the CEO as deployment leader, traveled to each of the company's dozen plants to conduct LEO overview classes for all of the company's employees. They knew that the deployment was in the works, of course, but the overview was intended to give them some facts to replace the gossip and rumors—and some reasons to be happy about the initiative. They were nervous because earlier corporate makeover projects had led to personnel cutbacks, and they were relieved to hear that LEO was focused on rooting out waste, not people.

INTO THE TRENCHES

With the completion of the training phase of the deployment, the time had come for the project leaders to embark on their assignments. The deployment leadership in each plant stood ready to coach them through the preliminary stages.

At the flagship plant, Paul was back managing his production line, just one of seven in the huge Art Deco building that dated to the mid-1930s. The LEO assignment was on top of his normal workload, but as was true of most project leaders, the project was physically located on his line. He could do the Listen phase of LEO right in his own backyard.

Typically, he chose to pursue his project—to fix whatever was causing a high rate of product rejections—on his own, without the aid of any graduates of the team member classes. Other project leaders often used one or two of the team members to take notes or keep detailed records of each step of the project.

Those records were entered into the company's existing internal electronic system. From the start of the deployment, a record of each major step was entered into that portal, from the earliest ideas for projects through the actual LEO project implementation. When a project was successfully completed, that documentation, along with the project leader's estimate of the money saved, would be presented to the finance people for approval. Meanwhile, the company would have a complete history of the deployment for future study in search of errors and best practices.

During the project phase, and, in fact, throughout the deployment, managers and frontline people were urged to try new ways of doing their jobs, to come up with new ideas and suggestions.

Part of the LEO mission of the CEO and his top executives was to encourage risk taking and out-of-the-box thinking—and to make sure that employees were not criticized for doing so. Supervisors were ordered to exercise patience with project leaders and project team members as they learned LEO in classrooms and while working on projects—and with the workforce in general, as employees found themselves expected to change their work habits and procedures because of LEO.

> **Part of the LEO mission of the CEO and his top executives was to encourage risk taking and out-of-the-box thinking—and to make sure that employees were not criticized for doing so.**

Paul was able to finish his project within a few weeks, and then he surprised us. He asked if he could enter the program to become a certified LEO trainer.

As I mentioned earlier, one of the company's major goals for the deployment was to make LEO an integral part of the corporate culture. For that to happen, for the company to continue using the system to achieve continuous improvement, would require a cadre of people who could take over after the initial deployment was completed. And they would require an extra level of instruction and experience leading to certification.

For anyone who is familiar with management programs like Six Sigma, the word *certification* will raise visions of long weeks devoted to a complex and demanding set of requirements. The LEO certification process is far less onerous, and it's also flexible, tailored to the level of knowledge and skill of the individual candidate. Basically, it calls for candidates to finish four LEO projects, including at least two that they have identified; show that the LEO system was used on all four; provide supervised coaching for two projects; and teach a project leader training course.

POWER OF THE DEPLOYMENT: THE CUSTOMER-CENTRIC CULTURE

The test of a LEO deployment's lasting power, its sustainability, takes place over years, of course, and this company's experience is too recent to judge whether it will pass that test. But there was at least one positive straw in the wind: the initial agreement with the company called for the deployment to end in 18 months, but that was extended for another six months in order to make sure that every one of the dozen plants would have at least one certified LEO trainer on hand to continue the classroom and hands-on learning process indefinitely.

Some months after the deployment was over, I once again met the CEO for dinner, this time in Washington, D.C., instead of Manhattan. He was in an expansive mood. The deployment projects had substantially exceeded the promised $85 million savings. Beyond that, the LEO problem-solving mindset had been widely adopted, assuring many more millions of dollars of savings over the years ahead. The customer-centric culture change that the CEO had sought was well under way. From my point of view, and his, mission accomplished.

But it turned out that he wasn't quite through with me. "You know," he said, "I'm on the board of a health organization in my town. Do you think LEO would work for it?"

I did.

With this chapter, I have completed my general tour of the LEO approach as a *business* strategy. In the final chapter, just ahead, my focus shifts to considering the advantages and challenges of the LEO mindset as a *personal* strategy. Among those you'll meet are a considerate surgeon and an apologetic president.

Chapter Ten

THE QUALITY
MINDSET

I n the summer of 1989, nine-year-old Melissa Poe and her mother had been watching a rerun of *Highway to Heaven* as they folded the laundry in their home in Nashville, Tennessee. The episode featured an angel warning that people might die unless something was done about the earth's air and water pollution. Melissa was moved. "I really wanted to help," she said years later. "I wanted to be one of those people who cared."

She sent a letter to President George H. W. Bush with some suggestions for fighting pollution. When she received no response after three months, she decided to act upon those suggestions herself. With the help of some sympathetic adults, a copy of her letter soon appeared on 250 billboards across the country.

Meanwhile, Melissa had started a club called Kids F.A.C.E. (Kids for a Clean Environment). Six of her friends joined, and together they cleaned up their neighborhoods, planted trees, and recycled cans, glass, and paper. The billboards brought in many more members and led to newspaper articles and appearances on TV shows. The club was adopted by Wal-Mart, and a Web site (kidsface.org) appeared.

As of 2011, Kids F.A.C.E. counts 300,000 members in 2,000 chapters in 22 nations. It has distributed and planted more than a million trees and organized a variety of national and international environmental projects. Melissa, now a mother herself, still does volunteer work for the organization that she began all those years ago.

How was it possible that a nine-year-old girl could accomplish so much? I think the answer is very simple, and very important. She believed that she could do it. She felt that she should make a positive difference in the world, and she went for it.

That's a challenge we all face. We can spend our lives just getting by—earning C's in school, telling our bosses what they want to hear, and shrugging off concerns about the neighborhood or the world. Or we can strive for quality in everything we do—at school, at work, in the home, and in the community. I believe we have no choice, as individuals, as organizations, or as a country. We must, like the young Melissa, have the courage to reach for the things and the standards that we believe in. Everyone can make a positive difference in the world.

We can strive for quality in everything we do—at school, at work, in the home, and in the community.

PEOPLE QUALITY

Yes, I've already talked a great deal about quality in this book. Most of that talk, though, has been about quality as it applies to processes—putting out corporate fires, developing ideas and solutions, and perfecting those ideas and solutions. Listen, Enrich, and Optimize. This chapter, however, is all about people quality.

For a LEO project to succeed, it must have the support of the company's leaders and of the managers and frontline people who are directly involved in the effort. But something more is required if LEO is to transform the company, allowing it to achieve unprecedented growth, profitability, and overall quality. It requires that the individual people within the company, leaders and frontline employees alike, acquire a high-quality mindset.

That same equation applies to any world-class organization. Just consider what has happened to Toyota in recent years. For decades, the company was the very definition of world class—individual quality wed to process quality. In 2008, it passed General Motors to become the world's leading carmaker. But within a year, its reputation and its sales were in tatters.

Battered by reports of crashes of its cars as a result of unintended acceleration, Toyota recalled 3.8 million Lexus and Toyota vehicles late in 2009—its largest recall ever, but that was just the beginning. The total was to rise to more than 11 million before 2010 was over, all because of high-speed incidents, including a fatal crash related to acceleration.

The company's process quality had clearly fallen, and it soon became clear that there were problems with its people quality as well. After the first recall, the *New York Times* noted: "Toyota faced

questions over whether it routinely fixed potentially dangerous defects in new models without recalling those already on the road."
The U.S. Transportation Department levied three maximum fines
on the company, for a total of $48.8 million.

"We now have proof that Toyota failed to live up to its legal ob-
ligations," said Transportation Secretary Ray LaHood. "Worse yet,
they knowingly hid a dangerous defect for months from U.S. officials and did not take action to protect millions of drivers and their
families."

The company's president, Akio Toyoda, apologized profusely.
Seeking an explanation for Toyota's malaise, he spoke of a growth
rate that "may have been too quick," suggesting that because of
this, "priorities became confused." In other words, among those
leading the company, profit was given a higher priority than performance.

Profit trumped quality.

The kind of dishonesty described by LaHood—any dishonesty,
for that matter—drives out individual quality. As you have seen in
the previous chapters, the LEO system is based upon honest data.
If the information gathered in the Listen phase of a LEO project is
false or misleading, for example, the project will fail.

Dishonesty . . . drives out individual quality.

For much the same reason, high-quality leaders understand
how important honesty is to their success and to the success of
their organization. Leaders like Alan Mulally, for example, the CEO
of Ford Motor.

Honesty

Mulally took over at Ford in the fall of 2006 after a remarkable career at Boeing. Since then, Ford has experienced a dramatic turnaround, recovering from years of huge losses to earn profits of $6.6 billion in 2010. By all accounts, the credit goes to Mulally.

I was fascinated in the spring of 2009 when *Fortune* wrote an in-depth description of Mulally's leadership style. Every Thursday morning at eight o'clock, he holds a management meeting with his direct top aides. There are reports from the company's four profit centers—the Americas, Asia Pacific, Europe, and Ford Credit—and from 12 people heading up different functions, including manufacturing and government relations.

One of Mulally's first requests after his arrival was that the reports be color-coded green, yellow, and red—for positive, caution, and negative, respectively. At the early meetings, the executives all showed up with reports coded green and full of good news. The boss finally lost his patience. As he told *Fortune*, he reminded them that the company had lost billions of dollars the previous year, adding, "Is there anything that's not going well?"

One of the executives allowed that there was some technical trouble with a new model, and when he was done, Mulally actually applauded, saying, "Mark, I really appreciate that clear visibility." By the following week, the reports were coded all over the three-color spectrum.

Honesty really is the best policy, for practical as well as ethical reasons. In a LEO project, the leaders have to be told the truth by the front line; otherwise, they will make decisions that are bad for everyone, from workers to customers to the executives themselves. By the same token, the leaders have to be straight with the frontline workers if they expect honesty in return. They must also make it clear that truth tellers will not be punished, since the fear of being penalized or fired is the most powerful enemy of honesty.

> **In a LEO project, the leaders have to be told the truth by the front line; otherwise, they will make decisions that are bad for everyone.**

The forthright relationship I've just described is part of the basic structure of a high-quality organization. In LEO terms, it's individual quality leading to process quality.

There is another value that is a key element of the high-quality mindset: empathy.

Empathy

A few years ago, a friend's wife had a pinched nerve in her back that was extremely painful. Surgery was required, and when that day arrived, my friend nervously paced the waiting room. After about two hours, his pacing was interrupted by a nurse. She told him that the surgery was still continuing, but that the surgeon wanted him to know that he had relieved the problem and his wife's pain was gone.

When I heard the story, I was blown away by the surgeon's thoughtfulness. Even as he was doing the surgery, he was concerned about the state of mind of the patient's husband out in the waiting room.

Normally, of course, you have to wait until the surgery is over before you get word of whether or not it has been successful. Up until that day, I had never even heard of a surgeon who followed this man's policy. And as my friend discovered in a later conversation, it *was* the surgeon's customary policy. When my friend expressed surprise, the *doctor* was surprised. It just seemed to him to be reasonable behavior.

Reasonable, yes, but all too rare. What he had done was to extend his empathy for other people to this aspect of his profession. It wasn't in his job write-up, it wasn't something that other surgeons did, but it was consistent with his standards for decent human behavior.

Empathy is a core value of the high-quality individual.

Like honesty, empathy is a core value of the high-quality individual. It is also an aspect of LEO because it enables everyone involved in a project, both leaders and frontline people, to better understand how customers and other stakeholders feel, the goal of the Listen mission. Again, individual quality breeds process quality.

Individual quality breeds process quality.

Resistance to Compromise

There is a third aspect of the quality mindset that I want to mention: a resistance to compromise. In their work, and in their personal lives as well, people with a high-quality way of thinking tend to be dissatisfied with results that others are ready to accept. They don't allow themselves to settle for anything less than the best.

Chantal Coady is one of those people. A chocolate addict as a child, she opened a whole new kind of chocolate shop in London in 1983 at the ripe old age of 23. Since then, she has never stopped looking for ways to raise the quality of her product and her organization while writing three popular books and transforming the world of chocolate in Britain.

Coady attended an art school as a teenager, but she was still feeling the pull of chocolate. When she took a part-time job, it was in the chocolate department at the elegant Harrods store in London. After graduation, she worked in an office for a while, but, as she told the *Wall Street Journal*, she found it "numbing and traumatic." That's when she determined to set up her own chocolate shop.

During her time at Harrods, Coady had been disappointed by the décor of the chocolate area and the lack of "emotional engagement" in the presentation. She decided that her new shop would be different—"a beautiful, sumptuous, theatrical environment." And as opposed to the department stores where most people shopped for candies, including chocolates, her place would sell nothing but chocolates.

Coady's shop, Rococo Chocolates, was an instant success, selling products made mainly by French and Belgian companies. Then Coady became aware of another whole level of chocolate taste and expertise. French chocolatiers were gathering cocoa beans from different locales—Indonesia, Latin America, and other areas—and blending them into confections based upon their individual qualities, much the way grapes from different vineyards were treated. By 1990, she was creating her own chocolates. Then she began mixing unprecedented flavors, such as geranium and jasmine, into her chocolate creations, an idea that was so successful that it was copied by major manufacturers.

Coady campaigned to convince the big candy makers to rid their chocolate goods of the hydrogenated vegetable fats and sugar that had misled the public into believing that chocolate itself was unhealthy. She went into partnership with cocoa growers in Grenada so that she could include in her product line chocolates that were fair-trade and organic.

There are three of her shops in London now, and Coady simply never stops coming up with new programs to involve her customers and attract new ones. She has established the Rococo School of Chocolate at one store, where classes in chocolate making and cooking with chocolate are offered for beginners and advanced students. It also hosts parties for kids and adults.

She sells, with the approval of a London cleric, guilt-free chocolate bars to people who have given up chocolate for Lent; half the price of the bars goes to support the church's Lenten Appeal. She arranges for the stores to host meetings such as a Women in Leadership Breakfast Seminar in connection with International Women's Day.

The list of Coady's initiatives is endless. She is tireless in her pursuit of ever-higher levels of quality. She has never come close to a LEO project, but she has the LEO mindset, always looking to Enrich her company's offerings and to Optimize them, to make sure they're the best they can be in meeting her customers' needs and desires.

That kind of individual commitment, I do believe, is the best hope for all of us—and particularly for our own country's faltering economy and industrial base.

A STATE OF MIND

As I have traveled around the United States, I have seen a different America. Once-flourishing communities have become ghost towns. People who were once happy about their lives and optimistic about their future are now despairing and fearful of what lies ahead. The nonstop wars in which the country is involved, the seemingly endless recession, the soaring unemployment rate, the foreclosures and bankruptcies, the unrestrained greed of so many banks and so many elected officials—those are some of the reasons why the average American is so discouraged.

We have a choice. We can simply accept what's happening and spend our energy groaning and criticizing, or we can, as individuals, try to make a difference.

> **We can simply accept what's happening and spend our energy groaning and criticizing, or we can, as individuals, try to make a difference.**

I wanted to do something to help, something that would give people a feeling of accomplishment while at the same time improving their prospects. It occurred to me that a different kind of LEO might do the job—a LEO that was totally separate from the corporate strategy version, tailored to the needs and aspirations of everyone.

There was a precedent. After the publication of *The Ice Cream Maker*, the small book in which I first introduced LEO, I received, out of the blue, a letter from John Richter, the coordinator of programs for youthful offenders at the Orange County Jail in Orlando, Florida. He described one of the jail's programs called Literature-

N-Living, which was led by a volunteer named Warren Kenner, a local Cingular Wireless manager. One of the readings that Kenner had assigned his students was *The Ice Cream Maker*.

As Richter pointed out, "These classes are not a cakewalk." Participants are required to write papers, take part in class discussion, and take a test at each meeting on what they've read. If they pass, they are entitled to a contact visit with their family members, who are also allowed to bring the prisoner a home-cooked meal. The letter included copies of some of the papers that the students had written, and it was clear that they understood the book very well, each in his own way.

"There is one thing I have learned that will help me if I apply it in my life," wrote one student. "That one thing is called LEO." Another excerpt: "Listen is the key when it comes down to anything. For example me, if I would have listened to my Momma, being that she's my internal and external customer at home. Not only I'll still be in business but it also would have showed her how important she meant to me."

When LEO was devised, it was intended to be of value to managers in trouble, not troubled youngsters. But as I mentioned earlier, the basic ideas behind LEO are simple and applicable in everyday life. They provide a template for intelligent, organized, data-based decision making in any circumstances.

> **The basic ideas behind LEO are simple and applicable in everyday life. They provide a template for intelligent, organized, data-based decision making in any circumstances.**

I remembered those letters when I considered how I might, as an individual, make things better in America, as well as globally. They helped in my decision to establish *Global Quality Awareness*, as it's known, which calls upon people to "Practice Individual Quality. Inspire Global Change." And the words of LEO that you have read so often in these pages now serve a broader purpose: Listen hard to others and to yourself; Enrich the lives around you by giving a little more every day; Optimize everything you do by setting your mind to excellence.

I believe that the LEO focus on individual quality that has worked so well for so many companies can also work for individuals and have positive effects on nations as well. The pursuit of excellence, and the commitment to quality, will set us on the path toward a brighter future. Dr. Seuss had it right:

Unless someone like you cares a whole awful lot,
Nothing is going to get better. It's not.

INDEX

ACKNOWLEDGMENTS

Without the significant contributions made by many people, this book would certainly never have materialized. For the development and production of this book I feel a deep sense of gratitude to

- A very special colleague and friend, Jim Quinlan, from whom I have learned a lot over the years. Jim, thank you for your hard work on the manuscript.

- Two very passionate colleagues, Brad Walker and Mike O'Ship, for their continuous support and hard work in improving the manuscript. Thank you.

- A great talent who helped me refine the manuscript with integrity and the highest quality, my friend Robert Stock. I feel a deep sense of gratitude to Bob for his enormous support and hard work.

- McGraw-Hill Associate Publisher Mary E. Glenn for believing in this project from the very first day I met her and for her encouragement in writing the authoritative first book on the subject of LEO.

- My editor at McGraw-Hill, Niki Papadopoulos, for her professional competence and project leadership—and for her continuous inspiration. A very talented and creative editor, Niki shaped the book from the day we first had coffee in a Manhattan restaurant to discuss the project.

- Everyone at McGraw-Hill for their hard work: Gayathri Vinay, Julia Baxter, Allyson T. González, Lydia Rinaldi, Zachary Gajewski, Pattie Amoroso, and Maureen Harper.

- All my colleagues and everyone at my firm ASI Consulting Group, LLC (www.asiusa.com) for their continuous support, promotion, and practice of LEO each day.

- All of my customers who have been enhancing my knowledge every single day since I started my professional career.

- My very special friend in the publishing business, Cynthia Zigmund. Thanks for continuous support and encouragement in all of my book writing.

- All of my readers around the world who have been the best supporters of my works.

This book would never have become reality without the support of my encouraging wife, Malini. Her continuous intellectual challenges inspire me each day.

Of course, the real joy in my daily life comes from my son, Anish, and daughter, Anandi. I hope one day they will embrace and practice LEO when they grow up.

ABOUT THE AUTHOR

Subir Chowdhury is Chairman and CEO of ASI Consulting Group, LLC, a world leader on LEO and Quality leadership implementation, consulting, and training. His clients include global Fortune 100 companies as well as small organizations in both the public and private sectors. Under Subir's leadership, ASI-CG has saved more than several billion dollars for its clients around the world. His latest organizational transformation philosophy, LEO, is successfully being implemented and employed by various organizations.

Hailed by the *New York Times* as a "leading quality expert" and by *BusinessWeek* as "The Quality Prophet," Subir is the author of 13 books, including the international bestseller *The Power of Six Sigma*, *The Ice Cream Maker*, and *Management 21C*. His *Design for Six Sigma* (DFSS) is the first book on the topic and is credited with popularizing the DFSS philosophy throughout the world. His books have been translated into more than 20 languages and have sold more than a million copies.

Subir has received numerous international awards for his leadership in quality management and his major contributions to various industries worldwide. He is an honorary member of the World Innovation Foundation (WIF) and has been honored by the Hall of Fame for Engineering, Science, and Technology, the Automotive Hall of Fame, and the Heritage Hall of Fame. He is the recipient of the Society of Manufacturing Engineers' Gold Medal, the Society of Automotive Engineers'(SAE) Henry Ford II Distinguished Award for Excellence in Automotive Engineering, and the American Society of Quality's first Philip Crosby Medal for authoring the most influential book on Quality. In 2009, the U.S. Department of Homeland Security presented him with the Outstanding American by Choice Award for his professional achievement and responsible citizenship.

Subir received an undergraduate degree from the Indian Institute of Technology (IIT), Kharagpur, India, a graduate degree from Central Michigan University (CMU), and an honorary doctorate in engineering from the Michigan Technological University (MTU). Both IIT and CMU honored Subir with their Distinguished Alumnus Award.

The London School of Economics (LSE) has established the Subir Chowdhury Fellowship on Quality and Economics, given to a postdoctoral Fellow each year to study the impact of poor quality on the advancement of economics of a nation, which is the first fellowship of its kind in the world. The SAE International has established the Subir Chowdhury Medal of Quality Leadership to be given each year to those who bring forth innovation and broaden the impact of quality in mobility engineering, design, and manufacturing.

The Subir & Malini Chowdhury Foundation is Subir and his wife's philanthropic foundation, which initiated a Global Quality Awareness campaign worldwide to raise awareness on quality in all spheres of life.

Subir lives with his wife, Malini, and two children, Anandi and Anish, in Bloomfield Hills, Michigan.